To ~~Mike~~

To Mike for all your d
Thanks for all you d

Best
Jim SPARKS

OPERATION MINDSTORM

STAFF SERGEANT JAMES SPARKS JR. MEMOIR OF DESERT
STORM AND HIS JOURNEY OPERATION MINDSTORM.

JAMES M. SPARKS JR. AND MELISSA SPARKS

authorHOUSE®

AuthorHouse™
1663 Liberty Drive
Bloomington, IN 47403
www.authorhouse.com
Phone: 833-262-8899

Published by AuthorHouse 03/22/2021

ISBN: 978-1-6655-2050-8 (sc)
ISBN: 978-1-6655-2048-5 (hc)
ISBN: 978-1-6655-2049-2 (e)

Library of Congress Control Number: 2021905998

For Jessica and Jennifer

Thank you, may life be good to you both,
if not don't "freak out"
Let go of what you can't control and
remember "Time is the true currency"

A special thank you to
Connie Humphreys, and Dr. A. F.

January 20,1991, this date is seared in my memory.

I didn't know it at the time that this date would mark the day MY WAR, the MINDSTORM, would begin. I was only 25 years old when I received the second generation Anthrax vaccine. This would forever change the course of my life.

I offer this book as testimony to how broken, disconnected and out of touch our VA system is with veterans. My hope is by sharing my experience, my research, my life, my war...I will help others who are fighting their wars back home. I never thought I would write a book right now just in time for the 30th anniversary of the Gulf War. I served eight and half years in the United States Army. My plan was to be a lifer until I received the Anthrax vaccine.

My decision to enlist in the United States Army came in the Summer of 1982. I lived in a rural community in Ohio; the economy was poor, and jobs were far and few between. I felt entering the military was my best option. I would be able to make a career for myself and my family. I was a part of a delayed entry program, a program that allows high school students to enlist while in high school, leaving for boot camp after high school graduation.

I learned I would be heading for Fort Knox, in my day the base was known as Home of Armor - for its training center and Armor school to train crews on M1 Abrams tanks.

In the spring of '83 me and the other new recruits were bused over from Cincinnati, Ohio, to Fort Knox, Kentucky. The bus ride was quiet, full of men around the same age. I was excited and nervous, but I knew this is what I had to do to make it in this world. It was raining when we arrived at Fort Knox. We were instructed to stand in formation all night long; there were roughly 70 of us, just standing in the rain, waiting for the next command. A couple of people dropped out the first night. I remember thinking "oh shit, what did I sign up for?" The next morning, we met the drill sergeant. I was exhausted and soaked with a lunatic screaming in my face. I knew better than to speak up, drop out or even give a sign that I was exhausted. To add to that I was still recovering from Mono. For the next 8 weeks, they pushed us to be the best.

I remember painting a portrait of my drill sergeant with fangs, blood dripping from them, on the floor of the barracks. I imagine this painting symbolized how we were all feeling. He was sucking the life out of us; pushing us physically and mentally. He was doing his job. To my surprise, he liked the painting. I never second guessed my decision to join. Boot camp was hard, but it had to be to prepare us to be the best possible version of ourselves. Quitting was never an option; it never crossed my mind. By the end of bootcamp, I was pumped. I was stronger than I had ever been, physically and mentally.

Following bootcamp, I was stationed in Fort Hood, Texas. I entered as an E1, in the military, E1 is an entry level rank. I found a sense of peace and direction. My job was to protect and serve the United States, this was my purpose, this is where I belonged, and I was good at it. I was driven to continue to be the best possible version of myself for not only myself and my family but for my country. I had never felt a stronger sense of belonging. I took every opportunity to learn and completed correspondence courses daily. I was promoted to Staff Sergeant at the age of 20. My job description was listed as 60 E40 – Tank Mechanic. I was a part of the 1st Cavalry Division.

In 1986, I was informed that my division was being sent to the Army base in Butzbach, Germany "The Rock." Our job was to collect surveillance, protect our interest, and defend the German people from Russian attack. We went on a mission to the border and back. There were certain cities in Germany that allowed us to get close to the border, something we were discouraged from doing. I took it all in. Since I was the mechanic, I had only one vehicle, a M113A2, and I was accompanied by a driver who was a Turret mechanic. I was never on a mission in Germany where my services were not needed. I spent 3 years in Germany, leaving in 1989 to return to Fort Hood, Texas. I was transferred from the 2nd Armored Division Tiger Brigade to 1st Cavalry Division.

Within a matter of months of returning to Fort Hood, I was receiving orders to go to war in Iraq. Adrenaline and training kicked in immediately, this is what I was trained for, this is it. I worried about leaving my wife and two daughters behind, but I knew that it was what

I had to do. No option, no second thoughts, only to push forward. Our unit was put on lock down as we prepared to deploy.

October of 1990, Our unit loaded onto a commercial plane leaving Fort Hood, Texas. Our layover was in Canada. From Canada we traveled to Riyadh, Saudi Arabia. The tension on the plane was intense. I could feel the adrenaline, tension and fear. The 12-hour flight was silent. When I got off the plane in Riad, the hair on my neck instantly curled up from the intense heat. I remember seeing desert for miles, no mountains, no vegetation, just sand and heat. From Riad, we embarked on an 8-hour bus ride to our base, Camp Melissa in the desert (which I thought was awesome as it's my wife's name.) We arrived at night; I remember being so cold. We had artic sleeping bags to sleep in at night because of the drastic temperature fluctuations. It would be 120 degrees during the day and drop to 60's at night.

Our days were spent running through the cliffs and valleys with our tanks, constantly training and perfecting formations. We would work through the war-time simulations like encountering the enemy and performing missions. In my down time I began journaling. We played football, wrote to families, I drew sketches. I sketched a picture of a fly, it was an 8x10 sketch and the fly was every bit that size. The moral of the base was welcoming, the soldiers were focused on their job and the task at hand. Most rose to the occasion, others succumbed to the fear, tension and pressure walking the line of insanity. One particular Staff Sergeant was gunning for me, literally. One particular soldier damaged his vehicle to avoid the road march. War can bring out the best and the absolute worst of mankind.

As we write this memoir I "his wife and now caregiver" have struggled with his story, mainly because they tell me a memoir is told in first person. My wounded warrior is not capable of this today! So the next chapter is his words. His journals from the first Gulf war. From there I will be a narrator to help him tell his story! After reading his journals multiple times, I think like most people who have been sent to war struggle with the ethical and moral dilemma of going to war!

DEPLOYMENT JOURNALS

October 1990, It didn't dawn on me at the time that maybe I wouldn't see my family again. Then they were gone as quickly as the Master Sergeant snapped us all to attention, "Right....face, forward march." We immediately picked up a step but it soon faded away as everyone's heart sank, as mine leaving the wives and children standing watching us head off to war. I was angry not only at the prospect of leaving a beautiful wife and two daughters, but also, angry at the idea of being herded like cattle. I was remembering the day early in the morning, when we dropped our bags on what looked like a cattle truck. Everyone's wives were with them; even though we could go home for a short while, the petrified wives were staying at their husband's side every moment they could. We had to come back later to be herded into the gymnasium to be processed for the flight manifest they call it. The HQ company captain was screaming to an NCO; they lost accountability of a soldier. "God dam it; go get him, find him, get him in the fucking formation now," the NCO scurried off to find his soldier who was in the back of the gym. The wives stood and watched. I know they had to feel sheer terror from the captain. My oldest daughter almost six at the time cried aloud. In the formation, heads turned towards us at the rear rank of formation.Their looks seemed to invade our little space - our last union possible. I resented that. We said our goodbyes as the Master Sgt. Hollered, "Pick up your gear; it's time to go." Some wives made their way to the gymnasium, catching last moments with their husbands.

This photo was snapped moments before we deployed.

We were stacked like cordwood on the gym bleachers, as tight as we could, to get everything orderly, only to look down after we were packed in to find the bleachers only half full. They called us by alphabetical order, "Get in that line; pull out dog tags and ID cards." Only as Army logic goes, the A's were at the top of the bleachers, so they had to crawl all over everyone else to get down. The soldiers were grumbling as they got stepped on.

We were bussed to the airfield, Robert Grey Army Airfield, West Fort Hood, Texas, and immediately loaded up on a 747. We were about to realize, in about 19 hours, that getting stepped on at the gym was the least of things to grumble about or worry about. Our stop in Canada was uneventful if you like $1 Pepsis. The stop in Frankfurt was a chilling experience as they had to unload us off the plane for maintenance. The night cold bit us hard as we stepped off the plane dressed in Fort Hood climate uniforms; it was Oct. 7th. I wished I could have stayed there though. I think the only time anyone looked out the small plane windows was when we were passing over the sea of sand below. We quickly landed. The temperature didn't seem bad, I guess anywhere on earth was nice after a 19-hour flight.

1ˢᵗ correspondence home

The next few days were sticky, hot, and very uneventful, as we waited for our ships to arrive to unload. The "tent city" as they called it, was full of rumors of hookers getting caught at the head of a 100-man line, of people getting not just bitten, but mutilated by snakes and scorpions. We tore down tents, and put up tents, moved from one tent to another to get things ``orderly.'' The showers were hand built of plywood and screen and pipe. They got particularly nasty after a couple of days.

We were warned, "Do not play football behind the latrine; it's off limits." There was a Saudi base there, probably an anti-aircraft battery, heavily fenced and guarded. "They will shoot you if you get too close." I tried to imagine one of our soldiers retrieving his football near the fence and getting too close and getting riddled by bullets because he looked like a threat. It was that good old army logic. We played football behind the latrine, which someone thought to put up wind of the tenants. And no one was shot for retrieving the football.

12 October 1990. The tanks arrived and we were getting tents organized for their arrival. The tankers, the ones who would be told to drive straight toward the enemy, never to expose anything but their front. They are a group of guys, put on their 60-ton monster, and required to perform the crew duties associated with keeping the tank rolling, shooting, and hitting, putting "steel on target"! My job along with nine others of my men, was tank company maintenance team, I was chief or as they used to call it, and still do the "motor sergeant." It's not an elite job, sometimes it's rather difficult.

The days passed under clear blue skies in the scorching sun; we were camped temporarily in a little piece of desert; we had received our vehicles from the port with minimal damage. Our company was chosen to represent the Army way of life in the desert of Saudi; the second platoon got the honor. I will probably always regret not going up to those reporters and telling them my story; however, I was ordered not to disclose any news but good news. Don't talk about parts supply problems nor anything that would be considered bad news, in other words don't say anything. I guess that was proven, by my opinion only, when the article was published in December 1990, "Platoon". It was a bomb and did great injustice to soldiers and the truth.

We were settled into our camp, semi-permanent camp, or "life-support area" they called it. I felt as if I was on a frontier no one had ever been. We completed chores day in, day out to build our life support area, showers, sinks, mirrors, latrines, tents were in a short supply. After a few weeks we were all tented. We were a growing colony of soldiers, trying to live and cope with one another, and with news from politicians arguing like children, stress was peeking and falling throughout the company.

We could feel it like the waves of an emotional sea; no one was exempted from the feeling.

1st pic camp "melissa" 2nd pic Jim Sparks rolling into tent city. (I think he looks like John Wayne – Melissa). Third pic life in tent city

20 Jan 1991 this I will learn was the beginning of my new war!

Some context here, Jim did not put this in his journal. He signed a secret statement and he held to that. He told me later he never put anything in his journal that would compromise their mission. However, I feel it's important to add. He tells me they were in Iraq on patrol when his Lt. S2 security came and told them to get their men and line up for a vaccine. Jim tells me it was their first base camp melissa (ironic). They had been up all night patrolling about 7 miles from the camp when he got the order. They had been in Iraq about 2 ½ months when the trucks rolled up with boxes of the first generation anthrax vaccine.

On this day the Captain said you are all getting Anthrax shots today. I went and told my crew, and we all lined up. I was next and was handed a clip board and told to sign my name that this was classified secret. We did as we were told; as this was the way of the military.

9 January 1991   0330 hrs.

"Wake up, we're moving, they got only S&P's to move APC's, you've got forty minutes before you go." I stirred and woke. The cold bit me as I rose from my sleeping bag, so I laid back down & got warm, checking

7

my watch every couple minutes. Ten minutes had passed. The XO called my name "SSG. Sparks, SSG. Sparks up there?

Yes sir, what's up?

"You ready to go?"

I barked, "Shortly sir."

"Well you've got five minutes; they've got SOP'S over there for you pointing in a Southeast direction."

"Five minutes," I hollered, as I usually did to the XO. Just because he's the messenger doesn't make him immune from getting barked at. I knew he could change more than he ever tried to but he didn't try so I didn't treat him as well as he'd like, but he continued being a messenger.

When I'd bitch about a higher up decision, he'd say, "I know, I know, but there's nothing I can do about it."

But I knew the rest of it. "Did you ever try to do anything?"

"Yes," he'd say.

I'd challenge him, "Honestly?"

"No," and we would both laugh. We both really did know there was nothing either of us could do. I was rebellious; it didn't help.

"Five minutes, JD says it's getting hotter up North."

I barked again, "What's going on, Xo?"

He says, "It's just getting hot up North."

"What kind of fucking intelligence do we have? Is that all they can tell us? Somebody needs to pull their heads out of their ass. Do I assume ammo?" As usual, I didn't get any answer. I knew people thought I had a bad attitude, not really bad but a rebellious attitude. I continued my barking with the hope that someone would take the same attitude and get some answers from the higher up. Once in a while I was satisfied at justification but not often.

9 January 1991   1353 hrs.

Well, five minutes turned into twenty some hours. The S&P's haven't arrived yet, and the Aziz – Baker talks didn't go smoothly. So, I decided to have my driver load M16 magazines. If the crisis ever ends – I'll get laid every day the rest of my life, and I'll be happy no matter where I am, except here. I will probably always regret leaving Melissa Ann, my wife, and my two daughters, Jessica Nicole and Jennifer Lynn. Melissa and I married young. I being 19, her being 15, but I'll never regret it. We've grown a lot together. She's a beautiful woman, five foot four 108 lbs. of pure joy. Brown hair to match her brown eyes. A strong jaw and a slight overbite that's very sexy. She's my complete opposite, wouldn't hurt a fly, easy going, fun loving, well to be, well to do type person, no enemies, I on the other hand am pretty complicated, ill tempered, stand my own ground type person. We've helped each other's qualities in one another. I've hardened her a bit; she's softened me. I wouldn't want a mate with the same traits as me; we'd never get along. She still remains faithful and loves me, even with all my faults

Melissa promised to stick by me through all this mess and forever. I believe her because she stuck by me when we were young. Just coming into the Army as a private first class, I married her in a small court room of the justice of the peace in Bell County, Texas. A small wedding ring which she still wears and won't give up for a larger one. A small apartment with cockroaches. She never complained, never does although she is starting to gain her independence.

My mom, she's where I get my firmness, she gave us five years then said we would divorce. That passed three years ago, now at eight years out plus. Mom and Melissa get along like sisters; they're taking care of each other through this crisis. Melissa is my dream of a woman, although she complains of being too skinny!! Kind of odd for a woman to say that...isn't it? I know I've got all kinds of things to share with her when I get home, things I've learned about life, through reading a great deal. I know she'll be fascinated at some new insights I'd like to use in everyday living, but I'll talk more of that later. I'm jumping ahead of myself. I still remember seeing her look of amazement at places in Germany, the Black Forest, the first time she saw the ocean, at the seawall in Galveston, Texas. The look on her face of joy and happiness to be alive; I want to see more of. We'll explore the world. We resolved to get out of the Army when my hitch was up, 2 July 1991.

If nothing else I'll regret not preparing for the future. All of our energies were put towards living day-to-day, or payday -to- payday. I had come home from work one day and told Melissa I'm tired; I want to get away from here. I was tired of daily routine, fighting with "higher up" about maintenance concepts, aspects, and the need for more. I was fed up and burnt out. I had just gotten switched from 2nd Armored Division and got transferred to 1st Cav Division, only to find the maintenance program a mess. I was highly recommended by my Battalion Maintenance Officer and Battalion Commander; however, when I found myself in this mess, I was a newcomer and couldn't penetrate the routine of my new peers or supervisors. Time and time again, we were given unrealistic time limits on missions, driving my tanks into the ground even before I inherited them.

13 January 1991   1730

We had just moved North about 100 Km or so East of the neutral zone. A fifteen-hour bus ride, our Pc's were on S&P trucker flatbeds. We set up behind a French outfit, who lit up the night with unorthodox tactics. We arrived – we were the maintenance tracks, medic trucks, and FIST truck. It was a rainy day getting colder each Km we went North. The rolling desert floor turned into a flat, desolate, and deadly terrain, as we would soon be storming across.

12 January 1991

1800 brief by S-2 / Colonel. "I feel no one wants this war. The Iraq's or the Arabs, nor the U.S. I looked for some sort of solution at the last minute; Saddam has been known to do one eighty." The S-2 seemed to be a quiet, intelligent man, a Captain whom I had briefly seen other times before. We (the Task Force) had only a few BFV and M1A1's pushed to us, a problem with heavy equipment transports.

The task force commander briefed me, being the senior man so far to come north from Bravo Company. "Have your Pc's ready to go to C Company if anything happens before we get our tanks. You'll have one hour to get them to Charlie." I went back to my 12-man company supply and medics, and maintenance. Put out the guards and tried to get some sleep. I didn't think much of what the Colonel had said. I didn't believe it would happen the way he did.

13 January 1991

I asked the supply Sgt to go to the 1500 staff update for me. I was muddy and wet because we had just put up the maintenance tent. The guys had asked me if we could put it up and get warm inside with the makeshift pot belly stove. I was reluctant, saying I didn't think we'd be there long. They pressed. We put it up and started digging in.

I was inside my PC butt naked except underwear reading a book. I didn't have a heater. I was trying out something new I recently read, that if you take all your clothes off and relax and concentrate you could be warm. It worked while I read my book. "Echo zero two this is Echo 9er two, get all units REDCON One, pack up, prep to move tonight."

We arrived at Charlie a few Km's across the flats. They had scattered fox holes. We drove through their perimeter toward the center where the tents were and the men, for they had no vehicles yet they were dismount infantry. They showed us where to park and we swung around and dropped the ramp. I took a good look at the men. Standing there in the cold rain with jungle boots on water sloshing in and out of the drain holes. Their huge rucksacks lay in the water and sandy-mud fear and excitement in their eyes! I dismounted and asked the lieutenant, "Where are we going sir?" We mounted our vehicles; the men packed in all seven grunts and their gear. We drove in wedge formation a few km's to the ASP; it was getting dark quickly, raining harder and cold. I couldn't feel it yet, my adrenaline was pumping. The rumor was shit is hitting the fan up North. We lost satellite communication and are anticipating a ground assault. The grunts had ten minutes to grab all the ammo they could carry. We had about twenty PC's in all – from the entire task force mechanics. I always envisioned maybe becoming infantry when all else failed and we were desperate. But now? Before the war even started? Loaded with ammo we drove fourteen hours Northeast 110 km. We didn't know what was going on, where we were, or what to expect, we didn't know if forces punched through the border or what?

We were all prepared, however very cautious. Early morning, we arrived and set up a coil defense and waited and dried and waited and dried for two days. (dried meaning dried out from the torrential rains.) All that time the grunts were ready and waiting, and could have done the job if needed. We talked about what had happened. I felt sorry for those grunts; they were a team, had to sleep on the ground, live on the ground and they didn't complain once in the few days we were together, unlike others. Our tankers arrived on 15 January. They had finally showed up. I was the happiest I had ever been at seeing tankers. The grunts would soon be on our left flank in the battle that would live forever in the history of mankind, and would change the world forever? Our mission was to defend KKMC, a military city very strategically located. If Saddam would take it, it would set our mission back 6 months to a year.

16 January 1991

Our radios were silent, except for the squawk of squelch, and an occasional weather update. My men pulled guard each night, a boring and aggravating but necessary job. The battle had begun; Iraqi's attacked a small deserted city where Saudi troops were unaware that the Iraqi's tanks came with their gun tubes over their back deck-an international sign of surrender. There they traversed their huge gun and started fire. First reports were 12 marines were killed then later it reduced to 11,. Reports are the Iraqi's took heavy casualties, 400 prisoners, over 200 dead as I write the battle continues. I searched for maps to locate where 4 divisions reported about 1000 vehicles,

60000 troops staged to attack again. The air force is bombing the vehicles now easier targets along a 10 mile stretch of convoy reportedly destroying over 100 tanks so far. The other night I heard and saw planes going over head, heading north lights blinking as they passed under the moon. Then lights out about 5 minutes later.I saw a missile launched in the sky apparently from a fighter. It streaked down; the flame disappeared 3 seconds later. I saw a brilliant explosion on the ground then another rocket fired.

17 January 1991   0200

I woke up for an operation order, very confused and angry at the ammo distribution priorities. I rose not at my calmest, so I took it out on the platoon Sgt. He's a good NCO and fair man; I regretted chewing on him. I apologized later. He briefed me on the OP order. I loaded our vehicle, came to red con 1 and tried to relax.

17 January 1991   0300

The radio squawked "guidons, black 6 break, red air has just crossed the border, scan the air, you may lock and load weapon systems, break, at 0400, start taking PV tablets every 8 hours, acknowledge" Red roger "Blue Rodger" White Rodger, This is black 8 Roger. I'll interpret what has just confused some people. Guindon's are platoon leaders, black 6 our company commander, red air enemy aircraft PV tablets are pre-nerve agent tablets, recently found that they help third stage nerve agent symptoms. This transmission was the first word of war we received and afterwards we received a flow of intelligence info to let us know what was happening.

Ten or fifteen minutes had passed; guidons red air had turned around and headed North. The ground movement was an awesome display of what would happen during an assault. On each of our flanks were army tankers, Pc's medic, Pc's M88's artillery, and Hemi's as far as the eye could see, moving in formation.

Intel update: the United States has started an air raid and bombing campaign. Approximately 100 cruise missiles were fired at Iraq and Kuwait. Catching them by surprise, evidently Israel announced Iraq is already devastated, probably because Iraq hadn't yet responded. We continue pressing North through dug-in units, support units, a city, and finally 50 Kms South of the neutral zone where we settled in and waited. I had my m88, dig in our vehicles and we continued until updates such as "high desertion rates from Iraqi's." 50 Iraqi tanks and 120 personnel defected to the Egyptian forces. The United States is still bombing, taking out scud launchers, which were like finding a needle in a haystack. We heard reports that the Iraqi's air force was dispersed in civilian population areas, knowing that Americans would not bomb heavily populated areas. We waited and went through all the scud alerts and so forth. So far, I was surprised. This is nothing like I thought would be happening to us during war. I imagined it at a faster pace; was I wrong? We could hear the impact of bombs due north and east. Our own artillery was registering not too far away.

19 January 1991   1200

Operation order - Mission when called upon 1-13 days after tactical bombing- move north 45 km's within neutral zone- set up defense be prepared to attack or defend -10 km south of forward Iraqi units....... I briefed my men. We waited, from what we heard the war was going our way, an 80% success rate in bombing. The weather was wet and chilly. We checked and rechecked vehicles, weapons, night vision devices, chemical equipment, and ourselves.

The Command Post (CP) was located on a small drift beside a Bedouin shack once inhabited, but probably deserted for fear of imminent war. It was partially dug into the sand and made of scrap wood and tin roof material, with canvas and cloth thrown over the top for a roof. With a makeshift corral in the backyard, probably for sheep, a bay of sheep bones was found outside. A wooden bed very roughly built was all that was inside. No bedding or anything worth living on. The staff used it for a place to shower. They hung a canvas bag up with a plastic shower spout fixed to the bottom. The weather remains cold and wet, unusually wet for a desert. Myself and my crew struggled each night pulling a three-hour shift a piece. There were three of us. It was getting to us so we started sleeping in the day partially. My back was getting in bad shape from wearing flak vets continuously, and especially on my 14-hour road march from hell with the infantry a week or so prior. We got our heads butchered to help hygiene.

The command Staff of B Co. got briefed by the S-2, a remarkable briefing and it would make world history. I'll explain after this ordeal is over, for I am now sitting in my track waiting. I do not want to disclose any info I may be captured with, so I'll lock it into my mind and write later. I will disclose, however, the briefing was at 1200 hours 21 Jan 1991, and like I've said it will be history. My crew and myself are figuring what we will destroy if captured: our radio, frequency and call sign book, and other misc. items. We have 9 cases of MRE's which are boxes of 12 meals, and we have about 30 bottles of water. I wish I were home, safe and happy with my family. I miss them so much I'm going to do anything I can to survive and complete this mission. God willing, I won't have to kill anyone. I'd probably regret it for a long time, but if I have to so be it, better them than me. I have a family waiting on me. I hear the thumping sound of bombs in the distance. I'm ready to head towards them and get this over with and go home.

22 January 1991

We've gotten three LAW's per track now, 900 rounds of 50 caliber, 180 rds. 5.56 a few incendiary grenades, star cluster, illumination cluster flares, and myself some .45 caliber for a pistol I carry. If I get close enough to use it, I'm in trouble anyway. I expect more ammo and some fragmentation grenades.

I've briefed my people."Make sure you do not break down. If you do you will be considered a casualty; this is war." Of course, I would not leave anyone for casualty. I would do everything to get them out, even if they broke down. My words did however give them a sense of urgency in making sure their vehicles were capable enough to make the journey they would soon encounter. It will be a long hard journey but very possible. We were instructed not to use heaters any longer to conserve fuel. We'd need all we could carry, and much, much more. We checked everything again, rearranged our vehicles and waited.

My biggest worry will be (is) artillery fire. The Iraqi's are regarded as having a formidable artillery capability; however, they can't seem to hit on the move, just predesignated targets. Another worry is indirect fire and infantry with hand held missiles, RPGs etc... The elite tankers could take care of anything else. My fears are about gone; however, I may feel different when things get hairy. I keep imagining a checker board of bullets screaming overhead. However, it will probably be slower paced than I imagine. Nonetheless I will keep my head down and eyes open. I am relying only on what I know and my faith to survive this conflict. If I do so be it. If I don't then so be it also. I did my service either way, and I don't regret joining the service or staying in for eight years. My grandmother was hysterical when I told her I was going to Saudi. She was the first to suggest the Army for me shortly after my graduation from high school. I was a womanizer. I did drugs. I had fun at others' expense. I regretted that part of my life. However, I feel back then I was full of energy and could live forever. I had some good times. Then I grew up. I still have fun but my energy has been zapped by the constraints of being an adult, taking on responsibility and being more reserved because of the effects on others from having a "good time." Some might say, "Oh he went to war and it took that to get him religious." That may or may not be the case; you decide. Since I arrived over here in Saudi, I've been reading a lot of "spiritual" material, not really religious, no, not at all religious in that sense of the word.

I've been into more scientific aspects of the human mind and body, the spirit, or the "self" or "I" as in who am I, where do I come from, and why do I (we) exist? I've been very intrigued by a combination of material I've picked up only by chance, and with plenty of time on my hands as a result of waiting in the desert for months. I am not a religious person.

I was fast approaching that time in my life where I needed an identity, a purpose. Like I said, I had decided to leave the Army shortly, and I needed something to identify me outside the Army as someone besides "Sergeant." With the job of Sergeant, you have little time to read or learn more about "self." You are usually preoccupied coping with problems of your family or your soldier's families. I remember many nights answering to the distress of either a neighbor wife or one of my soldier's wives. I had decided the pace was ridiculously fast and I couldn't keep up. I didn't want to keep up. I wanted to settle down, start a business or build a home, and live. It just so happens a war has drowned those hopes; however, I am changing myself for the better every day, and when I get home, I will continue to change to the lifestyle that suits me and my wife. I am sure she will find my new discoveries fascinating, as well as powerful. Everyone will probably go through this change in "his or her" life. I did not get religious at the outbreak of war. I was already ready and willing to change my life, and it has helped me cope with all this war stuff.

"Freedom this is Black 6. There will be approximately 10 slow movers flying through our area shortly, acknowledge." The Air Force was putting a serious pounding on the Iraqi's. The aircraft moved through our area about 2 minutes later. They sounded like B-52; the propellers buzzed through the sky overhead. Schwarzkop had wanted better weather, but the clouds and rain still persisted, evidently making the air force work a little harder. I heard impact to the north again; the B-52 were unloading their death on the unnerved soldier below. I could imagine bodies dismembered flying through the air and the concussion shattering vehicle and equipment and men's minds. I have wondered several times how men can always bring themselves to destruction for such firm beliefs that are dictated to them such as the Nazis, Jim Jones, and Saddam alike? Why would people be so far out of touch with reality and themselves are to be taken by the hand of leadership that would so casually take human lives? Don't call me a hypocrite. I know I am in the Army. This Army hates war. I hate war. Any soldier hates war and the ultimate sacrifice of retrieving their bodies for the cause. However, there must be some sort of rule in order in this world where a lot of people are out of touch with reality. Hell, I don't even know for sure if I am in reality ballpark. How come so many people are so confused about how to live? Why do bankers take advantage of people? Why do politicians lie? Why don't they realize that whatever they do that does not promote peace and good will, will be one day reversed upon them?

I've taken a good look at myself in the past couple years, and that's where I found all my answers. People should become aware of the reality of themselves, then they'll find answers as to why they shouldn't lie, nor do harm against humanity or nature. It's right in front of our noses and we miss it all the time.

If you have any doubts about what I'm saying, read *Out on a Limb*. She has had real insight and I am not going to ponder on the subject. I do not want to take anything away from her, nor *Dianetics*, nor the Bible itself. All above are excellent reading. They have not changed my life. On the contrary, they put things on the right perspective from three angles, one being scientific, one being spiritual, and one being "what can I believe as opposed to what is not proven by the other two angles." I can believe a lot. Some things I had a feeling I knew already, but I've forgotten over the years, or maybe haven't realized for a lifetime, but strange feelings of awareness passed over me. It's quite hard to grasp onto; however, one can keep an open mind and grasp onto anything, like the Nazis', or the Jim Jones followers. Did those people keep open minds and believe their leaders? I think it's high time we look to the right leaders and get back on track, I think, like I said before, we need to look into ourselves and to leaders who will guide us not toward destruction or hate, but towards peace, love, and the stars. We need to get real. Why are we here? Who are we? Where do we go? I'll bet people never expected to hear this kind of rubbish and they may not care for it, but just ask yourself who is leading you and where are they leading you to? In your heart do you want to follow these leaders on what path?

Being a soldier I have for moral reasons, questioned my leaders the same way I had to before I became involved in a campaign to kill other humans, and I feel at their level of reality, they are trying to do the right thing, so maybe their timing is off a little, or maybe this is the start of a new peace in the world that will last a millennium.

I hear impacts in the distance like thunder, only coming from the ground instead of the heavens-- are we co-creating with God, a more peaceful world.? Are we devils with high--tech weapons trying to conquer the world? -- highly realistic questions. Which is the realistic answer? I am not a conqueror; neither are the American people. We could all use a bit of spiritual guidance and awareness. It helps us with our purpose in life.

What did they scratch from our Bible? How much do we need preachers who lie and commit sins they so actively persuade us not to commit? They've made a lot of money preaching a partial message. I want the rest of the message. Who are they to censor the Holy Bible? Which part did they omit that is now the missing link to living in peace and harmony? There is a great mystery out there I want to solve before my time in this life ends, and I will pursue it. It's that strong and that real and that right. I am no one to say I have knowledge, but look around, do a little exploring, take time for yourself before you jump into a conflict, such as I have. It will help you in your struggle, whatever it may be.

I am not criticizing all religions for this crime that was committed many years ago, and I am sure I can find plenty of organizations out there to suit my needs, as well as my hopes and inspirations, but first I have to survive this ordeal.

22 January 1991

I've had to put my men out on guard. They are quite bitter about it, not by their words necessarily but by the way they express themselves. I arrived and took over this team in June of last year. They still haven't come to fully trust me. They were used to a passive, pushover type guy who let them have free reign at all aspects of their jobs. I am responsible for their lives, and since I cannot pull guard every night, I must give them the burden, for their own good. If things were not so hostile, if we were not at war, they know such things I wouldn't put upon them. I hope they can come to trust me soon, fully.

I listened to the news tonight. I took the Walkman Melissa sent me and spliced it to my vehicle antennae to get the radio station, but because of the length of the wire, and the way the frequency carried, I have to stand on top of my truck with the headphones on and face North. News is: Bush is really pissed at the way the Iraqi's said they would not treat POWs by the Geneva convention. They were being tortured, and put in locations as shields. So today was the heaviest bombing on the Iraqi's yet.

War does strange things to people. I feel fatigued, and my mind is emotionally drained every day. I feel bad sometimes, great other times, but I am keeping sane. I've got my whole life in focus and all I have to do is survive and make my men do those things they have to do to survive also. Today they all worked and worked on their vehicles. They reported to me they couldn't do any more to get ready, and I believed them. I have a feeling we will take some punches, but will survive intact. I pray that we will, and I have faith that we will!

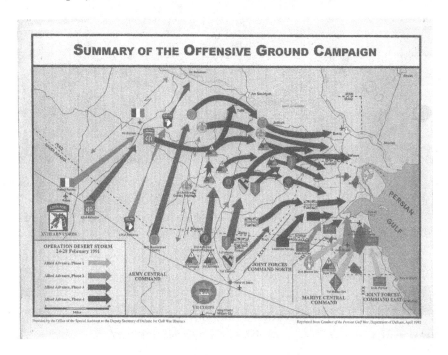

24 January 1991

We still haven't moved. The BBC reports two Iraqi jets have been shot down trying to penetrate gulf military shipping. They also report Soviet advisors are still in Iraq helping the Iraq Military. They probably are on their own. The soviets have nothing to gain from Iraq anymore.

I had decided to do laundry today on a limited water supply. I washed in two small tubs we also used to shave in. The bad weather has broken and it's quite comfortable today.

Saddam announced 90 military casualties to date, and said we were afraid to go on a ground war. He shall soon see who is afraid of whom. I think this guy is so full of shit. He pours out lies, and he probably does want us to go against him on the ground, feeling he is superior. Well he doesn't really know what we have in store for him. His soldiers and rapists do not have the air superiority they used to, and I believe he is really out of touch with his commanders in the field. They cannot fire artillery effectively, especially at a moving target. He cannot grasp the concept of mobility in armor, strike force, and shock action such as Patton used. He underestimates very badly.

24 January 1991

We had sliced turkey, peas, and carrots for chow. We became cold
from the walk back to our tanks. I reluctantly ate up what I could and
discarded the soggy paper plate. I heard a terrible grinding and someone
yelled, Stop the fucking tank." Second platoon Sgt. had just thrown
track because he made about a 90 degree turn to back into position for
the night (practiced daily they put them on line during the day, spaced
about 300 meters apart, during the night they moved into a coil for a
tighter position to guard). The crew worked till well past 2200 fixing
their track, and they used up most of the company's spare track blocks.

25 January, 1991

"1622-Red air expected between 1645-1730 Guidon acknowledge"

We were pushing through the gap made by the other division. Rockets artillery busted around my track, the M88 and other PCs were taking the same pounding. Foxholes and trench liner to the left and right, in front, all around, I was buttoned up, looking through the periscope. I heard artillery shrap metal hitting the sides of my PC. Impact tears up foxholes, and make us jog our way through the terrain. The terrain is laden with chemical mines, constantine wire, and a thick smoke layer quietly all around, making it impossible to see farther than 10 meters ahead, or the vehicle I was supposed to be following. Compass out, I tried to stay oriented north; I thought before long the artillery will stop, and it will be clear for a while, but first, we've gotta get through this gap, more artillery on front, to the right, more mines. A checker board of tracer rounds flew overhead. Are we in low ground? Try to stay in low ground. My mask was pushing air down my throat, hooked up to the gas particle unit, blower motor and filter unit, which forces air through hoses that connect to a coupling on the individual protective mask. With this unit, you get plenty of air; without you must expend energy to breathe. Not normally equipped on a PC, my driver and I hooked it up since we had an extra on our parts truck.

25 January, 1991   1622

"Red air is expected between 1645–1730, Guidons acknowledge," the commander's familiar voice announced on the company net (frequency). We took the V17 aircraft recognition panel off my track, a bright orange panel; on the flip side it was an off pink.

I guess the pilots could see the pink better than the bright orange; we were always told that anyhow. We wore the panel on the top rear of the vehicle so over fly boys wouldn't shoot us, and considering no enemy aircraft should come from behind, we put them on the back so as not to be seen from the front by low fast movers. During an airstrike, we would stop in place and be placed on yellow hold weapon status. The enemy would have trouble spotting us unless he was right on top of us. At such high speeds I guess it's pretty hard to see us. I was confident; For the time being.

25 January, 1991   1752

Operation orders group meeting B Co. We gathered inside the Bedouin shack. The night was quiet and cold, with the exception of occasional aircraft overhead, and not knowing if friendly or foe, because of the earlier warning. I had a feeling it was both.

Stayed long enough to get briefed and do some laundry.

The commander briefed for the following day's mission. We were critical on tank shaft engine oil for the M1A1's and getting worse intelligence reports. An enemy soldier on the southern front defected and spoke up. They (the commanders) threaten the soldiers with death on a daily basis, they get daily rations of rice, and there are trenches in front of them with gas and oil. Mines in front of them, then wire, mines, behind them so there's nowhere to back up to.

The Commander had picked up a leaflet from the bombing. I guess we dropped leaflets on the enemy apparently telling them to surrender, and they will not be mistreated, or something along that line. For the first time I felt sorry for the Iraqi soldiers, but I quickly got it out of my head for I know if I felt like that, I was as good as dead.

I still have a few of those leaflets the U.S. dropped.

The commander briefed us on our mission-- about the same thing we had been hearing for days. Saddam had reportedly executed his air force general because he didn't put any planes in the air, so he is dead and they put planes in the air. We heard rumors of an enemy pre-emptive strike. I wasn't worried, to be honest. The rest of the meeting we mainly bullshitted, and I told of what I had learned of chemical agent use and antidote. I had read that the small pills we had been taking were calcium to counteract third stage nerve agent poisoning, that the usual atropine only took care of stage 1 and 2, and that only about 34% of nerve agent casualties die. My confidence was building. The Captain and I discussed for a while about how badly the United States family was slowly crumbling. We agreed that the root of all problems was family, and I suggested we needed to start back at the basics again: spirituality, guidance, and a little discipline, but not abuse, which is too widely accepted today and should be ruthlessly punishable by exact reflection of the abuse to the abuser. We need to get back and focus on what America is all about. A highly spiritual union is what our forefathers intended; instead, we have a material society, with greed in high places, and morals only on the surface, like a mask.

I was guilty myself, and I thought back then I was moral. I had and still have a lot to learn.

26 January 1991　0437

I was awake, off the rack, woke up, got up, got dressed, went outside and pissed.

0445 drivers started the tracks at normal stand to. This was all a lovely ritual. 0500 I called the Captain, "Black 6 this is Black 8 over, Black 6 responded, this is black 8, green to green all elements red con one, over. This is 6 roger out." Mine was a short version compared to tankers, letting him know we were up, started, weapons accounted for, and ready to go on seconds notice Red con 1 we had another phrase we made up, called gripping or grip to stress or be stressing; we then modified that to grib con- we were grib con 1 sometimes. Trying to keep a grip on reality, gripping for our lives, it was a flexible term.I liked it. I gripped a lot of times; I wasn't alone.

26 January, 1991   0900

We hurried up and waited to roll, red con 1 again at 0900. We finally pushed north 50kms at 0940 or so. A huge mass of military equipment moving at once, dirt and sand kicked up into the horizon, looking to the left and right, nothing but vehicles to each horizon. Artillery, medics, PCS, M88, M1A1's, trucks, command post caravans, HMV's, even Apache warships and VH1's tagged along. Grenades and their Blackhawks watching their units, figuring out how wide their particular units front was while moving.It was a once and lifetime site, Awesome. Military machinery tooling through the desert, a whole division online and rolling, and turning, I could imagine Patton somewhere up ahead, directing tank traffic. He wouldn't need to this time; we were really trained.

We passed an M88 with a blown engine bellowing blue smoke, apparently it blew a jug or 2, maybe all 12. An M88, my first vehicle in the Army, 56-ton tank recovery vehicle equipped with a 25-ton hoist winch and boom.; A 90-ton main winch for pulling, a spade to stabilize for heavy pulls, we used the spade blade to dig many fighting positions, since we were last in priority for engines. Not its intended use but if damaged I wouldn't worry; I saw no need for winching out in a flat desert. I'd winch a tank out of a tank ditch maybe, but we could hook up and pull it out. The task force commander's intent is to use the M88's to cross through mind fields if nothing else is available. Instead of using a tank, he wanted tanks for combat power. I had to agree. Anything to help us win this war sooner. I am ready to kick ass and get home.

SECOND JOURNAL

I could imagine the pilots and bombardiers, strapped in their cockpits, scanning the radars and sights, seeing a good target, and they do their job of firing their ordinance, and relaxing, pulling out of the attack, and repeating this as long as they could Not knowing when and if they will ever land safely this time. It looks to be an exhilarating experience, something out of *Star Wars*. The whole war was high tech so far: smart bombs, laser guided missiles, heat seekers, clean shiny 20th artillery tech, doing a job of mass devastation. And hardly any casualties, except for the lurching few.

The fighters and bombers continued relentless striking, improving each strike with combat experience, and diminishing resistance. We are in the future, I feel. Patriot missiles smart enough to fire at their own command, tracking and destroying only enemy ordinance, so accurate and expensive, they mark the future of the so-called "Star Wars" SDI. I felt proud to be a part of this technological war. The aggressor is paying for his miscalculation. We all hope he will attack with those thousand vehicles. Our tanks have yet to prove their 20th century performance. I was skeptical, though, because since we got the new tanks, my job has been minimal. I was worried another movement may prove to be fatal for the company, if our technology started getting temperamental, as it sometimes did, and all at once. Maybe this time it would be in battle. We were rolling the dice, chancing on non[-] combat proven technology.

My job was easier, but the knowledge replaced the stress lost from the current lack of maintenance problems. We had a couple of problems.

Apparently, they were solved, or at least not coming up now. A couple of tanks are burning a lot of turboshaft oil. I contributed it to a break in period where the engine bearings need to wear in and seat better. I was hoping the oil consumption would stop soon. We were running extremely low on oil. No oil meant bad engines quickly. Within seconds an engine could destroy itself. Even though our technology had allowed for protective modes in their engines, it would only take a few seconds of having a dry bearing to cause disaster. The M1A1 Abrams tank engine has a variety of sensors that influence the performance and protect the engine. They include an oil preserve sensor-sensor oil pressure. If low, the engine aborts and will not start again until the problem is resolved. Speed sensors which measure the turbine shaft speed to influence fuel control, and air control temperature sensor (thermocouples) which monitor engine temperature continuously--engine temperature can change from 900 degrees to 1500 degrees within seconds and drop as quickly. If a certain temperature is reached, fuel will be restricted to a certain amount, to let the engine cool. Another sensor monitors outside air temperature or the temp of the air being taken in the intake. Same as a jet engine.

Other mechanisms measure and influence fuel input, air input, power input. The brain (electronic control unit) monitors all the sensors and commands fuel flow, or issues a protective mode if there is a problem. A very elaborate engine, and sometimes temperamental, a grain of sand could get into the air tank, and at a high velocity tear a chunk of a compressor blade, thus causing a chain reaction that could destroy an engine quickly. We checked and rechecked air intake systems and seals to measure no ingestion of particles. This was crucial to the tank's survivability and ours. The tank's turret, five control system and biolistic solution computer, along with a thermal imaging system to see clearly at night--were twice as complicated as the engine systems. I knew that's where we'd have our main problems. So far, we've been lucky. I pray our luck continues throughout this conflict. If we start having problems now then we are as good as dead, and Saddam would be pleased to see our technology start failing. The tankers had it good. A new tank and a nuclear, biological, and chemical protective system built into their M1A1 tank systems.

1 February, 1991   0045

The radio squawked on admin log net "Guindon's intel update follows each company answered, CPC channel answered and Iraqi division has closed with Iraq's 12 armored division, location North 29 degrees, 20 min East, 46 degrees-27 minutes. Near 12th armor." We called the company commander, told him to go on secure (green) and told him the transmission. A few moments later the radio squawked again. "T55's seen in the First Infantry Division sector significant activity increase up north." I thought we would be in battle by morning because they were due north. High command figured if they were to attack it would be during the Wadi Al-Batin to take the military city. Our job was (is) to defend and stop them in their tracks. We were about 2kil west of Al-Batin. I was confident we'd crush them if they tried it.

I slept peacefully without event. I woke up and we weren't in battle. At 8am the Platoon leader, Commander and myself went on recon; we took along the medics just in case. We took off like a bat out of hell across the Wadi Al-Batin, a hard bull road which we figured the Iraqi's would orient and punched south. We crossed the road and set up to defend K10, a small border patrol town. If necessary, we'd push them out if they tried to occupy. We reconned and returned without incident. Chow arrived. My system mechanic told me we should get the men together for a bitch session, sort of informal. I agreed and had him gather the men after they ate. They ate and came 2 by 2, or 1 at a time. We got everybody?" I asked.

"Missing Rob, someone responded.

Everyone finally gathered as I drew a map on the sand of the whole theater. I wanted to brief everyone at this opportune time, so I knew everyone would know what's going on. I explained where the ground battle had taken place, where we were, how many prisoners had been taken, how many Iraqi's were killed, etc. I then explained our mission and contingency plan. And tried to calm everyone down as best as I could. I tried to open the dialog. Major took the ball for a while. He was quite upset. He told the men, ``I am tired of you complaining and acting negatively. We have it good compared to some guys. You need to think about doing your job because I am going to do mine. I am wearing these stripes because someone trusted me too. If you guys stay negative no one's going to pull you out. I will, you can trust me, cause it's my job. I want to bring all of you guys home alive."

"I promised my wife and God I'd do my job and bring you guys home alive." He broke into tears and choked while he continued, "We're all we got. You guys are my family out here and we got to stick together. If we don't it's all over now, and if you don't like it go somewhere else. I am tired of hearing your complaints." We did have our share of complainers; the guys have been complaining of not getting mail calls and late chow. I even had a couple of guys complaining we would not go home and we'd fight the Russian's next.

I added my own words, "I am tired of the complaining also. If you think you got it bad, put yourselves in that girl's place, the one the Iraqi's got prisoner. Think about her. To me, she makes this mission worth all the hardships, and all the late mail, short water supply and eating cold chow. We could be in a lot worse shape than we are now. We could be up north dodging artillery. Look I know we were all brought together as victims of circumstances, but we've got to stick together and stop complaining about bullshit. We're in the biggest war since WWII. We are making history here. I don't want to remember the bad shit, only the mission and its importance." We all stood silent.

Everyone got the point, I think. I explained how the little stuff will get on our nerves if we let it. We need to think before we get angry or depressed and try to think about the positive aspects and our jobs. I have been doing a lot of calming down the same way, and I am staying sane. I knew some men still didn't trust me. I told them if shit starts flying, I wouldn't turn and run, and I said it to mean it and make it soak in. But I wasn't going to babysit. Impact, the hatch just shook, we have been seeing flashes of impact since we arrived at this location. I hated the prospect of killing anyone, for fear of a cosmic justice of a sort later on. I also fear and hope America will not get big headed over the current situation, and start cracking jokes over winning. It didn't seem appropriate. Someone, I don't know who, mentioned on the radio this could be the start of WWIII. I hated that prospect the most, if it were true. I feared not seeing my family for a long, long time. Am I losing touch with reality? I need a good ground? I've been away from civilization and the real world too long. I long to go home, with a victory, not too much bloodshed, and not having to kill anyone. I only want peace? Like I said peace? I must be losing it.

2 February, 1991   1910

I've got to take off this flak vest; my back is killing me. Another piece of intel, Egyptian troops laid to the North, snarling the road with 4 companies of tanks. Passage of lines were coordinated in case we had to pass through them. They would be recognized by their fuel tankers over the back deck. An orange panel on the front slope, and headlights on. God, I hope. This coalition strikes together. Iran has said they will side with Iraq if Israel gets involved. Russia wants an arms buyer to keep, and Egypt and Syria say they won't go into Iraq. We are living on thread of an already flimsy coalition. I thought why doesn't Israel give Palestine a little slack? I then thought a moment and then put the thought out of my mind. It's time to pull - radio watch. Again, killing with high tech weapons, holy war, WWIII, flimsy coalition, new world order, longest war since WWII, longer than WWII, chemical weapons, nuclear weapons. What I wonder is mankind going to do to itself in the near future? Why do we destroy ourselves? Why do we fight wars for peace? I questioned myself until I got a headache. My answers are that our mission is just, and we need a new world order. But who am I to answer myself, to rationalize my position or a potential killer of men, regardless of the cost-- does the means justify the ends? Who can answer me?

3 February, 1991   0700

The commander was about to start his meeting. I heard a faint buzzing; a prop plane was flying above us. A small unarmed drone plane flew right above us. The lieutenant was looking. Everyone kind of seemed stunned. Some obviously did not know we were capable of such equipment. After the explanation was given it was a small plane, with cameras etc. remote-control spies. I thought it was unbelievable that we are definitely beyond our time. I remember reading about the drones.

~~What would the Iraqi's think about this? What would they do when~~ they see this? Probably shoot it down and find it and claim a great military victory.

7 February, 1991   1307

I told the Corporal to go get a log pack. The first Sgt. was busy taking men to shower runs and the CO's HMM was taking him to a meeting. I decided to take my track. We launched off from our home piece of sand, traveled south, and I scouted about for our UNCP. Upon finding it we parked our 13 ton beside the battalion Master Sgt. truck. I dismounted, grabbed my mask, weapon, and flak vest as usual put on my Kevlar and went to find JD. I packed a wad of red muck and felt good. The corporal was with me and we waited outside the 577-command post for JD Thurman, the Battalion executive officer. He was a good ole boy; an aviation man, had a pacemaker. I respected him. Even though he'd like to say he's smarter when he's chewing you out. I at least respected his opinion. He came out and saluted before we had a chance to as usual. He likes to stay ahead of you at least two steps. He had something to say as usual. "What's going on guys? You fellas are doing a good job." He shook our hands.

"How goes the war?," I asked him, hoping to get good news. Like I said I respected his opinion.

"We're pounding the hell out of em. It won't go on much longer. We're cutting his logistics. Once you do that, you cut an army down to size quickly. These boys are a hurtin." I shook my head and agreed as usual. You couldn't do much else but agree. The guy talked like he meant everything he said. He was intimidating at times but I liked the guy.

1821--the radio squawked but I didn't hear it. Bring your units to red con 2. I heard several aircraft overhead. We were red con 2.

I called black 6, "]his is black 8 over."

"This is black 6 over, could you say again message over.

"Roger--alias to our east report in engaging enemy PC's. Report 200 enemy PC's in depth moving towards their positions. We will let you know if anything progresses, over."

"Black 8 roger-out."

We waited; we wanted to see something. My driver told us he saw aircraft putting out flares to avoid anti-aircraft missiles. Intel report update--friendlies report engaging 2 PC's another 200 moving target indicators coming from the same direction--type vehicle unknown.

8 February, 1991   1200

An Army psychologist gave us an anti-stress briefing. He was pretty good; he was a decorated Vietnam Veteran. He explained how we would see people do things we have never seen: Puking, pissing their pants, shitting their pants. We'd see body parts strung up hanging in different positions. We would experience the taste and smell of death. A taste and smell we would never forget. We would form friendships unbreakable and form friendships forever among ourselves. He used a bunch of psychological mumbles to describe what would be our minds afterwards. At least for some of us. 1 out of 10 he said would experience Post war disorder of the mind. I had already programmed myself to snap back into reality if I felt myself slipping away. I need to experience all this and do it consciously without losing touch. In other words, we men are shocked by something or are scared or unconscious. I believe they are most vulnerable in that their mind will shut down to a certain point, and your mind will block out certain experiences at the time of trauma. It will then react at a later date without consciously knowing the trauma is at work. That would continue until the trauma is experienced and remembered consciously. This is my best explanation and only an opinion.

I have a different opinion spiritually; it runs parallel with the scientific explanation and may be more similar than I know. I figured during the period of trauma when the mind shuts down the spirit may very well be seeking shelter or be chased out of his home for fear of what is happening. My strategy is to keep in touch with my mind and not hide and let my spirit experience what is going on. It's really hard to explain but I feel I am not alone in this type of thinking. Some other people are much more qualified to explain it. I know I am not a scholar, I'm just an average guy struggling to get through this war alive and somewhat sane. The waiting has got to be the hardest part or maybe not. Fear is the hardest part. Not fear of the enemy or fear of dying, the fear of God. Is there a moral justification for this war? Can we rationalize killing people? I've turned this around and around in my head. Call it lack of faith if you will but who can justify killing or condemn killing, only God knows that answer. I actually cheered the air force on then realizing that people, humans are dying. I sometimes feel ashamed and guilty and sorry for them. God please let this war get over.

10 February, 1991   0840

The Platoon leader, the Commander, the 1st Sgt, Platoon Sgt, and myself, and Doc rolled up to the TOC command post. They were dug in a makeshift shower strung up out in the open. Sandbag bunkers are scattered throughout the camp. We dismounted and bullshit a bit. Then we walked over to the send table. Engineer tape and string and labels made up our route north. This was the plan for our big battle. We were there to receive a logistics briefing. As this battle would be a logistical nightmare, we all had to be in tune, in sync, conserve our supplies and most importantly be mechanically sound. For this will be a long journey and would (or should) end this war with Iraq. We were approximately 2km west of Wadi Al-Batin and 30klm south of enemy front-line troops. 1st Infantry division would make a breach on Iraqi's defense farther west, 3rd Armored Division, and 1st Inf Div. holds it open, an eight-lane gap through Iraqi's defense.

The three divisions would travel five hours, stop, refuel, sleep, and rearm if necessary, travel 5 more hours (North), stop, refuel, sleep, and rearm if necessary (if we had made enemy contact). This procedure would go on until we reached the first of the Republican guards. We would have 1st Cav 37 medevac choppers and LRP basically a checkpoint for maintenance problems, and medical ambulances etc. every 10klm along our axis north. If something broke, we'd take it or limp it to the next CP north and drop it off. When we stop every 5 hours the last CP, we passed would have our supplies, fuel, medics. The 1st Sgt would have to go back and get it, bring it up to us. We'd have 2 hours to refuel and rearm and get the trucks back to the CP so they could resupply for the next stop. To give you an idea of one fuel consumption alone, it was calculated at 20 thousand gallons every 5 hours of travel. And this is only one Battalion of many. Probably 20 or 30 Battalions. Fuel would decide the fate of our mission at least theoretically. We wouldn't know precisely until our mission was over. They designed two task force size units: one to have bullets, the other fuel. Food--we'd have to carry all our food. They would not be able to haul it. Also water--the same, we haul it. If we had casualties, we'd have to medivac them back to the last PC. They would be picked up there. The dead would also be evacuated. No hasty burials are authorized. If the dead were contaminated by chemical agents, we'd have to decontaminate before we evacuate them. POW's same evacuation procedure, back to the last PC. Once we made contact with Republican guards, we'd have 3 options. 1-stop early and let them come out of their holes and get us, actually we'd destroy them, 2- go in three dug in position and flush them out. 3- go around the first division and cut off their supply routes and starve them out. Options 1 & 3 were preferred. We didn't want to take heavy casualties by going head-to-head in their defense. But first before the great battle, the other plan, the deception plan. We were to deceive the Iraqi's as to where our breach would be along their defense front. We are to create a 6-lane breach further east of the actual breach on the 13th of February.

10 February, 1991   2300

An artillery raid was introduced to the Iraqi's. Apparently in the fake breach zone the night north horizon was glowing orange. Earlier we had gone over our plan. We would depart current positions and move north to the Iraq-Saudi border to form a 9-12 ft high berm made several years ago to separate the Iraq-Saudi border. We arrived at 1700 to defend the engineers and artillery that would raid the Iraqi's and breach the berm. The scouts and grunts reached the berm. The engineers move up, set their explosives in the berm, for 6 holes. The grunts and engineers would run south 1klm, blast their holes, then run back up to their berm. Then 6 engineer bulldozers would carve the rest of the lanes flat.

Artillery-- a whole battalion,3 batteries were to hit predesignated targets CP's and GSR after the breach.We'd wait until 2000 hours while the deception team would put up some decoy tanks and watch. We were hoping some defectors would see the breach and come through the holes. But the intent is to deceive the Iraq's making them think we were coming through there. It sounded good. We'll see if it works. The Iraq's have already moved a couple armored divisions up there. We'll get them to build up more and then go around. They'd never catch up if they tried; that's where the air force comes in. I might also mention when we do our real punch, the marines will also do amphibious landing. Other marine divisions will punch north.

The alias (Arab) forces will punch north to the east farther and the 18th airborne corps will protect our left flank up in Iraq. Just like Powell said our plan is simple; first we'll cut them off and then kill them.

12 February, 1991

Dearest Melissa Ann, how is it going. I am doing ok really. Did you hear we got a tax break; no federal taxes are being taken out? I also heard some Congressman proposed a 10 thousand bonus for all Desert Storm soldiers, have you heard that? As you might know we are doing really well in the war. We have air supremacy and to date we've destroyed 750 tankers, 650 artillery pieces and over 600 armored personnel carriers, about 20%, that's good. That doesn't count what is broken down, which I figure about 10-20% more. He's really hurting and Bush will make the decision as to when we go in. That's good also because that means fewer casualties for us. It will take a little longer, but it'll be worth it. It won't be that much longer though so hold on and stop worrying. We have got the edge over this guy. I know our battle plan but I can't tell you. I will tell you it's a good one and we will beat this guy with few casualties. You just have to support us and keep the support back home for a little while longer. I need you to write to me now more than ever. I love you and miss you. My tanks are holding up good. We got new ones so we are in good shape. I hear bombs and artillery every day and night. All going on them, not on us. It's kind of hard to believe this guy can only fire scuds. He tried to attack a small town with a battalion of men and tanks. The Saudi's and marines wiped out that whole Battalion and took only about 17 casualties. They are saying 7 of 11 marines were hit by friendly fire.

12 February, 1991

Our 13th Feb deception plan has been put on hold (on order mission) probably because the president has put ground offensive due to interest in keeping casualties low and the fact that the air campaign is going well or so they tell us.

13th February, 1991   1815

The sky was getting dark and the missiles left their launches in waves. I saw the missiles engines ignite then a pause before the missiles jumped up and north. Bright white lights streak from the ground up and across about half a minute later to the north. Anti-air craft artillery lit up in small red explosions half a minute more than we could hear the explosions of the missiles hopefully hitting their targets.

About 20 minutes had passed then a burst of missiles left their launches followed by about 20 or so larger white lights which launched slower and I assumed were the larger missiles. One by one they launched, streaked across the sky for a few seconds, and were out of sight. The display was awesome. 12 missiles could take out one klm square grid on the ground. This attack was to take place at G-day 9. So, the countdown to G-day has begun. Of course, unless the higher command had shuffled around the timing of each operation. We wouldn't be told that much yet.

15 February, 1991   1500

The task force is moving in a wedge formation, A company took the lead; D Co took the left flank; C Co pulled back to provide rear security; B Co had the right flank. Once the artillery was set, the bomb landed the berm along a 200–300-meter area. The gun sounded off a loud sonic boom. The projectiles whizzed over our heads whistling to the target. The berm lit up and mushroom clouds came up. No return fire. The engineers then moved up, placed their chargers in the Berm to blast holes in the obstacle. I wonder about the Iraqi's reaction. What did they think was going on? Why did they not return fire? We observed while the deception team put up the decoy tanks. We waited hoping for defectors. Some spot reports turned out to be friendly troops walking around. We turned back south. It was dark-- really dark and the dust kicked up from the tanks blinding me even further. Even with the PFC-7's night vision goggles, I could barely make out the back of tanks as they screamed south. We followed as best we could while the 3rd platoon covered our rear. It's kind of odd how people fear the unknown. We all feared what was about to happen. Taking return fire and direct fire and landmines but no one really thought about the fear when we were in the middle of it. It was easier than expected. The Iraq's apparently knew something we didn't or they were no match for us. They may have had a thing or to up their sleeve but we didn't understand them yet.

17 February, 1991

Tri border region purpose deceive enemy for large operation mission. Move along axis B Co will not cross berm support 3-82 artillery 1/5th mover across berm penetrates enemy forward recon north. Estimate strength deceives the enemy and makes them think we are penetrating through defensive positions at the border regions. 2-8th Cal found they could locate mines with thermal sight because of temperature variances on the ground. Change mask filters. 1/7 took out an OP received artillery fuel counter battery took out enemy artillery. No friendly casualties. Destroy enemy radar towers. At least 2 tanks, 18th airborne corps got hit by helicopters. Garlic smell equals blister agent. Vehicles flag red equal wounded. Yellow equal NBC (nuclear, biological, chemical) green equals maintenance problem. 2 water cans per man.

18 February, 1991

The company moved out to link up with 3-82; their whole battalion would support 1/5 mission. 1/5 moved across the berm with Bradley fighting vehicles leading. They were an infantry battalion. Their commander gung-ho about infantry leading the way. They lost a vulcon and a couple Bradley's to anti-tank guns. They should have led with tanks. They wouldn't have taken any casualties. They took prisoners and did some damage but mainly they woke us up to the reality that we will make mistakes and take casualties and the fact that the Iraq's could shoot. They killed the vulcon with a 100mm gun, first round turret hit. The vulcon was beside the commander's vehicle and was too far forward especially since it was an anti-air craft weapon. We were upset at the casualties but like I said it woke us up even more. This is real shit. A 2-way gunnery. I and others wanted revenge for the hill.

The Iraq's got lucky this time. Next time they will pay. Should we have tanker casualties? Hell No! We were on a deception mission and a recon, and some fucking gung-ho infantry commander wanted to lead with infantry, light armor, not knowing what to expect. A big mistake and it cost at least one life. No excuse could replace that life. We should have led with heavy armor and a vulcan should have never been in range of desert fire weapons. I was pissed off. The time is over for gung-ho fucking infantry commanders. But the mission was successful and the enemy deceived.

19 February, 1991

I hear talk of the Soviet peace plan. I am skeptical; however, I hoped it would bring peace. I really don't want to kill anyone or be killed. On the other hand, I don't want Saddam to get away with all he has done. We've come this far and to stop us now would be a waste. I'm balanced between two points-one being the cost of lives for peace or peace for the sake of lives. I opt the cost of lives moreover. The cost of one life, Saddam.

I hope someone will finish him off soon. I didn't have much time at this point. We were prepping, checking, re-checking equipment, making plans, doing more deception missions. The Commander got us all together and read a tanker's prayer:

> All mighty God who is the author of liberty and the champion of the oppressed hear our prayer. We the men of the armor force acknowledge our dependence upon thee and preservation of human freedom. We know our strengths come not from our machines or ourselves but from you. Go with us as we seek to defend the defenseless and free the enslaved. May we remember that our nation whose motto is In God We Trust expects that we shall acquit ourselves with honor that we may never bring shame upon our faith, our families, or our comrades, grant us wisdom from your mind, courage from your heart, strength from your arm, and protection by your hand. We seek your special protection for our families and friends as we perform our duty. In your name, Amen.

We waited for the next mission. The high command apparently had mixed opinions on where we would penetrate Iraqi lines. Either by a frontal assault and if successful we would continue north. Or stay in place and move only if need be through the breach to the west or around the flank of the mind fields and entrenched Iraqi's. Farther to the west up in the foothills of Iraq crescent shaped mountains. We did not know for sure what would happen next. We could go anywhere and do any mission. We waited but I wouldn't say patiently. The whole mission was timed, planned perfectly; nothing could interfere with the war plan as to throw everything out of sync. Desert Storm was at hand.

24 February, 1991

We broke for the border that night, waited, and penetrated the berm. We crossed the berm for the first time looking for the enemy feeling out the front liner. Re-coning scouts were forward observing with power scopes and trained eye contact. Artillery sounded behind us. We moved forward slowly and continuously through minefields. A tank hit a mine and I saw the explosion. I told my men earlier to stay in my tracks. Within moments I saw from a distance the hell we were approaching. The radio squawked intel update. Re-con has revealed the following.

I saw a tank T-55 scorched black gun tub drooping still pointing north as if fleeing. Around it lay stakes and wire along the border. Mine fields, a trench, more trenches, more mines, our tank which hit a mine lay there in the field up ahead on the horizon. I saw flames licking out of the ground black smoke was in the sky.

Apache warships shot targets; 3 missiles coming straight out along the horizon for a distance then dropping to their target. More Apache's, more smoke artillery impacted to the left front of my track about 200m away. MRLS shot their payload by the dozen. Artillery impacted on the horizon. The fire trench flames were getting larger. As we drew closer, they shot 15-20ft in the air billowing black smoke, more trenches, empty bunkers, empty ammunition craters left behind bunkers and more artillery. We bypassed the mine field to the left as one tank from our company cleared a path to retrieve the tank with its mine plow. I saw an Iraqi grave in the smoke. We were about 2000m from the trenches. 2 trenches one each showing a strong point of Iraq defenses. If we were to go between them, we would be in Iraqi killing zone. Triangle shaped defense. Two strong points up front, one in the rear center connected with trenches, guns and infantry. We received fire from anti-aircraft. Artillery pieces were trying to shoot an apache. Third platoon called fire on Iraq troops and bunkers ahead. DPICM (dual purpose improved conventional munition) showered ahead. Artillery rang my ears. Our battalion shot a couple bunkers and troops in the open then spread out to show a large force. Phase 2 of deep strike 2 was complete. Now we'd withdraw. We had fooled the Iraqi's confirming their belief we'd come from that direction. We weren't full enough to go into their kill zone and besides our mission was to deceive. Our mission was successful. The Iraq's started mobilizing and missing forces along the border. We took no casualties but one on the way back-- a stray DPICM bomblet hit our artillery track.

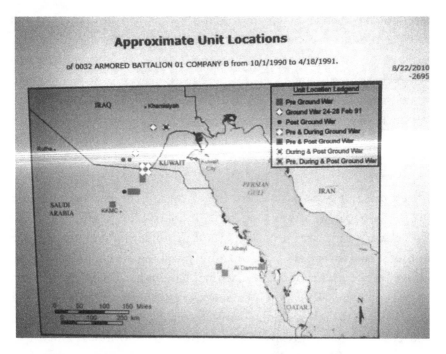

Jim is the top row middle

We had pulled back beyond the berm and lined up to make a left hook around the Iraqi's defense to the left. We stopped only to re-supply, regroup and rest. The Chaplin told me, "God had said the war would be over the 28th." It makes sense especially since the way the war is going now. The vehicles started rolling, miles of combat vehicles one behind another in convoy. We moved west all day so it seemed. My vehicle started leaking oil and it turned out to be the fill cap that was left open. We refilled the oil and caught up. My recovery vehicle was left somewhere to the rear at a support unit getting a new engine. I prayed that no vehicle would break. They didn't, at least nothing major.

I felt a sense of awe and it struck me to come to reality and look and realize, visualize what was happening. I looked into the distance at the fog of war to the northeast at the tanks thundering and spitting out tons of sand at every angle, at the guns searching for enemy targets, at myself, at the center of a war machine. I thought of helping to free a trapped person in Kuwait. I looked at the enormity of this project and then I laughed out loud and a smile beamed on my face. I was alive and enjoying being involved in something so enormous. Huge and the prospect of helping better the world, even if it cost me my life, tickled me. I felt a burst of energy that would last until the war ended. Energized, I could feel myself come alive. I could have run through a brick wall in stride at that very moment. The time was at hand. I threw my entire soul into this, no way to stop now.

We stopped in the foothills of crescent-shaped mountains in Southern Iraq. The mountains surrounded Iraq from the north and on each border. Descended to these foothills gently rolling green grass covered it. It Was magnificent, beautiful, and breath-taking. I knew I was on Holy land. Biblical visions flashed in my mind of shepherds and children and stone walls and farm animals.

We broke the fresh grass tearing a path for destruction, yet it was so peaceful, so serene, so quiet even with the tanks clunking from maintenance checks, chatter of men., and engines running. Yet, this whole division in this vast area seemed so insignificant. Quiet. We were parked in herringbone fashion, each vehicle off to each side of the road and at a 45-degree angle. The open road allowed access for HMMV's to go up and down the column. I climbed in a hummer with a friend. We went looking down the line for a couple of bolts that I needed. I couldn't sleep. We remained there for 3 or 4 hours. I was still pumped up more than just an adrenaline boost, I imagine. We ate and I argued with the XO about anything, as usual. We proceeded northeast from that point and crossed the Iraqi border at night. The berm had been busted by someone else: we simply went through a pile established breach with an array of lights, and marchers pointed the column in the proper direction. It was dark at this point. I couldn't even actually see the berm when we passed it. I took over driving after the 2nd fuel stop. It was still dark. We had stopped at the fuel point so I dosed for what I thought was only a moment. When I woke, we had only just re-fueled and started to move. I took over driving. The terrain was perfect. Gently rolling hills, green smooth, quick for our tracks everything was in tune, timed, and it seemed to be going too well.

Nothing is impossible, I guess.

3ᴿᴰ JOURNAL

S addam has tried to intimidate us using his propaganda. "You will have to live with the snakes and scorpions," trying to scare us; hell, we'll kill the snakes and capture the scorpions and have scorpion fights. Evidently Saddam never tangled with a bear before. However, from all of the reports his army is nothing to underestimate and there is a real chance of maybe getting wounded or worse. I thought about dying and death.

I wondered if there is a heaven or a spiritual plane of existence or if God is Spirit or human state of mind or hell a UFO pilot. I wondered if we'd live again or if I have lived before. One thing I know; I believe there is a God. Who or whatever God is…I recollected a poem from my past, from high school? As I was a dreamer and probably still am; it's only buried away below all the growing up.

A lot of moral questions pop into my head. Hell, I didn't even know what a Muslim is. We have so many religions in the world. Are they all wrong or maybe off base? I'm not a real religious person. I know and have known who leads me, protects me. I have quite a personal relationship with God. He gives me signs to let me know I am protected and of course I go astray sometimes as most do. Let me tell you a little short story about what I mean: a friend, a school friend and I went on a journey hitchhiking to California right after graduation. I went to see a girl I knew; he went I guess to give me company. Anyhow, sitting in a bus station in California, San Diego I believe, a young Spanish lady approached us while we were sitting on a bench. She handed us each a card, blessed us and walked away. Behind us we both turned our heads to thank her or at least stop her to explain. It hadn't been 5 seconds. We were out in the wide open on a bench. She was gone. We read the cards. "Jesus, I have written my friend's name James Sparks in the book of life." Another experience was in 1989 my Grandmother passed away; I was surviving in the last year of a tour in Germany. I asked my commander if I could go for the funeral. He got it approved. I got a space available flight on a military charter. I flew into St. Louis. I left the airport and began hitchhiking about 10 miles out. Two guys picked me up in a beat up old green car. One had a crew cut the other wore a baseball cap and looked kind of goofy, I guess. They started asking me religious questions...you know Do you believe in God, have you been saved, do you want to be saved? Etc. I answered their questions with hesitation and I felt quite odd in the situation. They took me to a truck stop 10 or 15 miles down the highway, pulled in the parking lot and shut off the engine.

The driver with the crew cut asked me if they could pray for me before they let me out. I hesitated feeling very strange then finally agreed to their wishes as long as they were friendly ones. They had me join hands with them. The driver prayed while the other guy sort of pushed him on. Then the driver started talking in a foreign language in which I didn't even recognize. A couple minutes passed then they stopped. The driver looked at me with a huge smile and said he truly believed I would be okay and someone would pick me up from here and take me to my doorstep. I was bewildered. I thanked them and departed as quickly as possible. That night a truck driver picked me up and drove me 600 miles to my brother's house insisting all the way. Even when I told him to let me get off at the exit of the interstate, he wouldn't. He drove clear to my brother's house.

He was very distraught with his wife when he picked me up claiming he was going to kill her. He showed me his gun, an old 22 pistol. When he dropped me off, he was satisfied with himself for helping someone out. He was more peaceful; he was smiling.

The End, well this is the end of my journals and the Gulf War ended February 28, 1991. Though the Gulf War ended, my war, the Mindstorm was just beginning....

I arrived back to Ft. Hood, Texas, July 1991. It just so happens I was due to re-enlist for another 4 years or ETS. My decision was made; I planned to leave the service not wanting to fight another war. I received a letter requesting I re-enlist. My current rank was E-6 Staff Sergeant. The letter made promises of a promotion to E-7 Sergeant First Class. One of the requirements when you ETS (exit the service) is to complete a medical exam which I did. At the time, I did not realize how important this exam would become.

Below is me telling the truth upon leaving the Army checking their boxes telling them the health problems I was feeling. I stated I was in poor health!

REPORT OF MEDICAL HISTORY

1. LAST NAME—FIRST NAME—MIDDLE NAME
SPARKS, JAMES MURRELL JR.

5. PURPOSE OF EXAMINATION — ETS

4. POSITION — SSG

7. EXAMINING FACILITY OR EXAMINER, AND ADDRESS — PHYS EXAM SVC, DACH, FT. HOOD, TX 76544-5052

8. STATEMENT OF EXAMINEE'S PRESENT HEALTH AND MEDICATIONS CURRENTLY USED
1. I'M IN * POOR HEALTH JMS
2. I AM NOT TAKING MEDICATIONS AT THIS TIME. JMS

13. WHAT IS YOUR USUAL OCCUPATION?
63F 30/40 Maintenance Team Chief

14. ARE YOU — Right handed ✓

DATE	SYMPTO...S, DIAGNOSIS, TREATMENT, TREATING ORGANIZATION (Sign each entry)

SOUTHWEST ASIA DEMOBILIZATION / REDEPLOYMENT MEDICAL EVALUATION

HT	WT	B/P	P	TINE TEST Date Done:
69"	184	100/60	72	Date Read: POSITIVE NEGATIVE (circle one)

1. What diseases or injuries did you have while in the Southwest Asia region? *Diarrhea, Stomach pains*

	YES	NO
2. Are you receiving any medicine, or other treatment, at the present time?		✓
3. Do you have fever, fatigue, weight loss, or yellow jaundice?	✓	
4. Do you have any swelling of lymph nodes, stomach, or other body parts?		✓
5. Do you have any rash, skin infection, or sores?	✓	
6. Do you have a cough or sinus infection?		✓
7. Do you have stomach or belly pain, nausea, diarrhea, or bloody bowel movements?	✓	
8. Do you have any urinary problems such as blood or stones in urine or pain and burning with urination?		✓
9. Have you had any nightmares or trouble sleeping?	✓	
10. Have you had recurring thoughts about your experiences during Desert Shield / Desert Storm?	✓	
11. Do you have reason to believe that you, or any members of your unit, were exposed to chemical warfare or germ warfare?		✓

Soldier's Signature _____ Date May 1991

attach audiogram ere.	500	1K	2K	3K	4K	6K
R	20	10	10	15	05	30
L	25	10	15	15	10	30

PATIENT'S NAME: SPARKS JAMES M. SEX: M
RANK/GRAD: SSG/E6
DEPART./SERVICE ID NO: 289-70-2695

Overprint Approved by USAPPC, April 1990
File in front of corresponding SF 88 and/or SF 93.
HSC OP 21-R (OT)(HSCL) 1 Mar 91

My official ETS (exit the service) was July 2, 1991. Melissa, my mom, and my daughters made the long road trip from Ohio to Texas to pick me up. Melissa and I upon getting the news of me going to war made the decision that she would pack up our small two-bedroom apartment and go home to be with family. The United States had not been to war since Vietnam; we had no idea what we were facing.

The war didn't last long and now I was back in our home town Greenville, Ohio, with dreams of starting a new life as a civilian. As for most things, it didn't go as planned; my dreams of starting my own construction business failed. We were struggling financially and emotionally; we filed for bankruptcy.

I was struggling, my marriage was rocky and we were now receiving food stamps just to get by. I was having trouble sleeping, and I had a rash on my face that would come and go. I developed lumps on the trunk of my body. I developed large patches on both calves of my legs along with stomach issues and fatigue. My hands and arms were going numb and tingling, often waking me while sleeping.

Melissa had finally had enough! While most of these symptoms might be chalked up to depression, she knew better. She will tell you I'm a type A personality, driven, and competitive. I was never one to complain or get sick. I scheduled my first appt with Dayton, Ohio, VA Hospital; the first visit was Aug 1991. I told them of all my symptoms. I had the usual tests, labs, x-ray and received a referral to mental health. One of the doctors told me there were no sick Gulf War veterans. Mental health chalked my symptoms up to readjustment to the civilian world. One doctor's appointment led to another and a referral to dermatology. My rash on my face was finally diagnosed as seborrheic dermatitis ("exact cause of this is unknown... certain diseases that affect the immune system increase the risk of developing")

https://www.medicinenet.com/what_triggers_seborrheic_dermatitis/article.htm The dermatologist was baffled by the patches on my legs; they tested me for a variety of diseases such as Lyme disease; most appointments they would bring in the students interning at the Dayton VA to have them look at my legs. However, I still had no answers. Other than the Dermatitis diagnosis and that my white cell count kept coming up high, I continued to go to doctor appointments. By 1993 I asked, which is documented in my records, if the Anthrax vaccine or the nerve agent tablets (Pyridostigmine bromide PB tablets) that we took every eight hours was the cause of my symptoms?

By now I had discussed my concerns about the Anthrax vaccine and PB tablets with Melissa. I told her how in the middle of the hot desert there were boxes of the Anthrax vaccines loaded on a personnel carrier and how we all were told to line up to get the vaccine, and that we had to sign a secret statement not to disclose the vaccine. It raised concerns for me at the time, but we were told we did not have an option to take the shot. I told her how I didn't write about it in my journals because I took the signing of the secret clearance seriously.

Melissa began to do her own research having never heard of Anthrax or an Anthrax vaccine. For those reading this born after 1990 you have to remember we didn't have the internet, computer or cell phones. Using encyclopedias, she found anthrax is a serious bacterial disease that affects sheep and cattle. She contacted a local veterinarian and asked about anthrax. They explained while rare that they were aware of a vaccine for cattle but not humans. She didn't get far with them. She contacted the FDA; they told her the last time the anthrax vaccine was studied for human use was 1940. They advised her to call Wright Patterson Airforce base located in Fairborn, Ohio.

We were starting to believe something happened to me and the other guys who served in the Gulf War. I was still going to doctor appointments and at one point a doctor told me I should file a claim with the VA. He stated it would open the door for more testing. I filed my first claim in 1993. Feeling desperate I went to a civilian doctor located in Cincinnati Ohio. He diagnosed me with chronic fatigue syndrome. I was insisting to the doctors at the Dayton VA on more tests to get answers. One of my 1994 medical records states "denial of testing due to lack of historical findings." I was, however, diagnosed with carpal tunnel as a result of the complaints of the numbness and tingling I was having in my arms and hands. This was B.S. but I'm getting ahead of myself a little. We'll come back to this later.

1994 it's now been two years since I began going to the VA. Melissa and I were doing everything we could to keep it together. I had decided to go to college to get a degree in engineering. She was working as a receptionist. We pushed through day-by-day. I was doing well in school except for my attendance. I received a warning every quarter with threats of being kicked out for missing school. I was juggling my health issues, working part-time and attending doctor appointments.

We came across an 800 number to call regarding "Gulf War Syndrome." We received the following response:

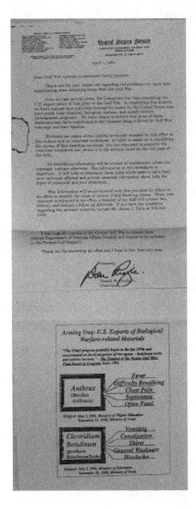

To save you a little time the summary of this letter states: The US Gov may have helped Iraqi chemical and biological missile-system development programs. Please fill out our worksheet, this will help us determine which units were most affected and exposed. He also gives a copy of a report he submitted showing the chemicals we sold them, and tells Gulf War Veterans to contact their local VA hospital to be included in Persian Gulf Registry. https://www.gulfweb.org/bigdoc/report/riegle1.html

We were stunned by the report from Senator Donald W. Riegle Jr. I know it may now be a bit of dry reading, but we were glued to it at the time. Were our worst fears validated? A member of Congress sends us a report stating he believed we may have not only been exposed to chemicals, but our own government sold the chemicals that they tried to protect us from. In comes the contract with the BioPort Corporation, based out of Lansing, Michigan. I'm getting ahead of myself again and will come back to Bio Port.

After receiving the letter from Senator Riegle, I did contact the Dayton VA Hospital and found out there was such a thing as the Persian Gulf Registry. I signed up! Again, receiving a variety of doctor appointments in the mail; lab work, x-rays, and yes, mental health appointments.

I went to all the scheduled doctor appointments seeking answers. Each appointment brought hopes of getting answers to why I felt as if I couldn't keep up with my peers. *November 3, 1994, I received the following letter: I participated in their Persian Gulf Registry; "the letter below says I am in good health." Really just another disappointment, no answers!*

DEPARTMENT OF VETERANS AFFAIRS
Medical Center
4100 West Third Street
Dayton OH 45428

November 3, 1994

In Reply Refer To: 552/136A

James M. Sparks

Dear Mr. Sparks:

We sincerely appreciate your recent participation in the Department of Veterans Affairs Persian Gulf Registry. This effort will help us to serve you and your fellow veterans who are concerned about the possible adverse health effects of exposure to toxic substances while serving in the Persian Gulf.

As was discussed, the results of your examination and laboratory tests indicate that you are in good health and have no reason now to be concerned about the possible adverse health effects resulting from exposure to toxic substances. If you have any questions or concerns about your Persian Gulf Registry examination, please contact the Persian Gulf Coordinator at (937) 268-6511 x 1073 for assistance.

The VA shares your concern about any toxic substances used during the Persian Gulf War. There is research underway to learn more about the possible long-term health effects of the Persian Gulf War.

Please remember that this examination does not automatically initiate a claim for VA benefits. If you wish to file a claim, please contact a Veterans Benefits Counselor at 1-800-827-1000.

The results of your exam will be maintained by the VA and will be available for future use as needed. If you have a change of address, please contact the Persian Gulf Coordinator at the number listed above.

Again, your participation in the registry is appreciated.

Sincerely,

In 1994 I also received my first denial of benefits from the Department of Veterans Affairs. I appealed the decision in 1995. I claimed service connection for Persian Gulf War Syndrome, undiagnosed illness and exposure to environmental agents.

I continued to try and provide for my family and continued going to the VA Hospital to try and get answers for my health problems. Each medical appointment brought hopes of answers only to be let down.

There was an occasion that the doctor told me we can't find your medical record (this was before electronic records). So, I would have to start over and explain all my symptoms. After leaving that appointment and going to the window to check out from my doctor visit. What do we see? My medical file was piled high on a cart! There were times we would just sit in the parking lot after an appointment. Melissa cried on a few occasions in frustration with the system.

1997 I thought there might be a breakthrough. The doctor was again trying to resolve the numbness and tingling I had been experiencing in my hands and arms. The doctor didn't tell me at the time, but because I would request a copy of my records, I found that he stated, "Symptoms of Lhermitte's Phenomenon Emg shows mild bilateral carpal tunnel which would not explain the Veteran's sensory complaints." I never believed I had carpal tunnel, and I refused the surgery they wanted to do on my wrist. I didn't believe it because I didn't feel my symptoms were typical of carpal tunnel, and by now we had very little faith in the VA System.

Over the next few years, I continued to try and better myself. My new career was taking off, but there was always this weight / battle. I was fighting to keep up with my peers. Feeling frustrated I went to see the local Veterans rep. I told her about my health issues and claims. She looked me up in their system and found my appeal from 1996 had been approved. A 10% disability rating for anxiety. I spent the next year arguing with the VA Regional office that I never received the notice. Then we received the following letter below:

DEPARTMENT OF VETERANS AFFAIRS
Regional Office
1240 East Ninth Street
Cleveland OH 44199

January 12, 1998   In Reply Refer To: 325/212A/GK

JAMES M SPARKS JR   SPARKS, James M

Dear Mr. Sparks:

This is to acknowledge your telephone contacts of January 7, 1998, and January 9, 1998. As a result of your telephone contacts and review of your claims records, it has been discovered that our decisional letter of March 15, 1996, was returned by the Post Office and no attempt was made to remail this letter or to acquire a current mailing address. We have redated this letter to protect your appellate rights. If you wish to disagree with any portion of this letter, please state the specific issues you disagree with.

Please disregard our letter of January 9, 1998. *wrong date — no letter exists with this date should be December 29, 1997.*

If You have Questions

If you have any questions, call us toll-free by dialing 1-800-827-1000. Our TDD number for the hearing impaired is 1-800-829-4833. *If you call, please have this letter with you.*

Sincerely yours,

Service Center Manager

Enclosure(s): Letter dated March 15, 1996 (redated January 12, 1998)
              Rating Decision
              Form 4107
              VA Form 21-8764
              VA Form 28-1900

cc: ALG (2)

It basically states that their decision letter dated 3-15-1996 was returned to them. Therefore, they redated the letter to protect our appellate rights. Please disregard our letter dated Jan 9,1998. Confusing, right?

This felt like a win to us for the moment, but the fight wasn't over. We were frustrated to say the least about the care or lack of care I was receiving from the Dayton VA. Once we received a copy of this decision, they actually stated, "denied for numbness and tingling of the arms, treated for numbness diagnosed with tendonitis." I was never diagnosed with this nor treated. All we could do is laugh but at the same time feeling so frustrated because you can't call and say, "Hey, you're way off base. You have to appeal their decision and wait on average (at the time) one to two years. So, I did what I could and appealed their decision. Sept 8, 1999, I received the following letter:

DEPARTMENT OF VETERANS AFFAIRS
Medical Center
4100 West Third Street
Dayton OH 45428

In Reply Refer To:

September 8, 1999

Dear Gulf War Veteran:

You are invited to consider participating in a study for veterans who served in the Gulf War. Following the deployment of Desert Shield and Desert Storm in 1990-91, a number of military personnel developed an unexplained complex of symptoms, which have come to be known as Gulf War Illness. While the cause of these symptoms is unclear and is being researched, efforts are being made by the Department of Defense and Veterans Affairs to find ways of alleviating the symptoms. Now the VA Office of Research and Development is leading a $20 million effort with the Department of Defense (DoD) to conduct two separate studies of possible treatment for symptoms of the undiagnosed illnesses of Gulf War veterans.

One study, which will involve volunteers at VA and DoD medical centers across the country, will test the effectiveness of antibiotic treatment in treating illnesses reported by Gulf War veterans. One current theory is that infection with the microorganism *Mycoplasma fermentans* causes the symptoms reported by Gulf War veterans. Some veterans have reported that the antibiotic doxycycline helps in the treatment of their ailments, however, a large-scale scientific study is needed to test this therapy. The other study will focus on exercise and a form of behavioral therapy that teaches techniques for reducing the severity of symptoms. Recent evidence has shown exercise and group processing is effective in reducing symptoms for patients with Chronic Fatigue Syndrome and Fibromyalgia, which have similar symptoms to Gulf War Illness. Our research is being conducted to determine if these activities will aid those suffering with Gulf War Illness.

We are contacting everyone entered on the Gulf War Registry at the Dayton VAMC to ask your assistance with this important research. If you were in the Gulf War theater between August 1990 and August 1991, have fatigue, pain or short-term memory problems, we urge you to contact us. If you qualify for either study, you will have an opportunity to participate in a supervised research study and be a part of a group of veterans with similar symptoms.

DD214   -10AM-   7th Floor North
7C 139
Maher

Desperate for answers, I participated in the research study which was to last for 19 months. It would consist of blood draws and me taking a pill every day for the next 12 months not knowing if I received a placebo or the antibiotic doxycycline 200 mg. I was required to return to the clinic once a month for the next 12 months. At the end of 18 months, I was required to return for another blood draw.

To this day, I have never received any answers from this study!

2000 We managed to keep our marriage together and find joy in raising two daughters: Jessica the oldest and Jennifer. Melissa continued to work for a nonprofit agency and was moving up in the company. I was working as an engineer. We would joke at times that we felt like we were living in the show *The X-Files* as technology was taking off; it opened doors to other Veterans who were suffering. Gulf War Syndrome became Gulf War Illness and now there was the Internet. I created a web-site wanting to share my experience, questions, and concerns with others. One day it crashed. We couldn't help but feel a little paranoid. We learned there are over 250,000 Gulf War Veterans that are sick. This was some validation. The VA was good at telling me it was all in my head. They even prescribed a few antidepressants over the years. I hated the way they made me feel and would stop taking them. I was suffering from extreme migraines that felt like an ice pick was being shoved in my eye over and over.

At this point I was begging the VA to do an MRI, having asked them many, many times. Up until this point I was given many excuses: one was it's not medically necessary. Another doctor said, "We don't want to go fishing for things." Another excuse was, we don't have an "MRI on site"; another time, "It's expensive testing." One of the Doctors even notes in my medical record, "Patient seems obsessed with medical testing like MRI" Well hell yes!! It may seem unbelievable now; most people can get an MRI rather easily today. It's the truth and documented in my medical records.

We were a young couple and never had to deal with doctors hospitals; the Veterans Administrations' red tape only made things 100 times worse. We were stumbling along trying to navigate the system with the goal of getting answers to my health issues. I was threatened on a couple occasions that they would call the VA police because I was upset, demanding answers. Actually, while at the hospital for an appt. they called the VA police. They were cool. Nothing came of it except I'm pretty sure my file was flagged. Melissa and I often laughed about the anxiety rating as we felt the VA system gave me anxiety! March 3, 2000, received a decision letter DENIED. May 16, 2000, submitted appeal.

I did seek outside medical care once again. I went to the kids' doctor in our hometown. He was a Veteran and the local coroner. His diagnosis to me was you're fucked up. He didn't put that in my record. I didn't continue to seek medical care in the civilian world. We didn't have health insurance most of the time. We fought like hell to climb back up from the bankruptcy. We even managed to buy a fixer-up home. Every extra penny went into updating the home. I didn't want to lose what we fought so hard to call home. The girls were growing up and doing well in school. When I wasn't working or writing appeals to the VA., I was researching what happened to so many Gulf War Veterans; was it the PB pills, chemical exposure, the anthrax vaccine? I received the following letter.

The letter dated 12-5-2000, below was an update to the exposure of Khamisiyah, basically extended the area of those who were exposed to chemicals but now states exposure will not lead to long-term health effects?

OFFICE OF THE SECRETARY OF DEFENSE
1000 DEFENSE PENTAGON
WASHINGTON, DC 20301-1000

SPECIAL ASSISTANT
TO THE SECRETARY OF DEFENSE
FOR GULF WAR ILLNESSES,
MEDICAL READINESS, AND
MILITARY DEPLOYMENTS

James Sparks

December 5, 2000

Dear James Sparks:

As the Special Assistant for Gulf War Illnesses, Medical Readiness, and Military Deployments, I am responsible for evaluating potential health impacts of your service during the Gulf War. I am committed to investigating and providing you with the most up-to-date and scientifically valid information available regarding the demolition of chemical agent munitions at Khamisiyah, Iraq on March 10, 1991. In 1997, my office announced that some Gulf War veterans may have been exposed to a very low level of chemical agent resulting from this demolition. You did not receive a letter then because our analysis showed that your unit was not in the potential exposure area. Since that announcement, more information has become available, and we have worked hard to improve our knowledge of the potential exposure areas and unit locations. As a result of these ongoing investigations, I am contacting Gulf War veterans, like you, whose units were near Khamisiyah March 10-13, 1991.

Using state of the art computer modeling technology and more accurate unit location data, we have improved our analysis of potential exposures to individuals whose units were near Khamisiyah during the demolition of Iraqi weapons. The models now predict that if you were with your unit at the time of the demolition at Khamisiyah, you may, indeed, have been exposed to very low levels of chemical agent for a brief period of time (less than 3 days) after the demolition. It is important for you to know, based on current medical evidence and ongoing research, there is no indication that any long-term health effects would be expected from a brief, low-level exposure to chemical agents that may have occurred near Khamisiyah.

I have enclosed a fact sheet that outlines our analysis, as well as answers to some frequently asked questions. If you have additional questions about any of the information that I have provided to you, please call my office at 1-800-497-6261 or visit our website at www.gulflink.osd.mil. Your local library may be able to assist you in getting information from our website. If you have specific health concerns, I encourage you to seek medical assistance from the programs established for Gulf War veterans. The Departments of Defense (DoD) and Veterans Affairs (VA) both offer comprehensive medical programs for Gulf War veterans. To schedule an appointment with the DoD program, call 1-800-796-9699; to schedule an appointment with the VA's program, call 1-800-749-8387.

We have a national obligation to protect the health of our veterans. I am committed to ensuring that you have the best information and healthcare we can offer.

Sincerely,

•Enclosure

We were there. We received a second letter in 2005 like so many other Gulf War Veterans, stating we are at a higher risk of brain cancer due to the exposure of low-level chemical warfare agents from "the demolition of chemical agent munitions at Khamisiyah." We blew up the chemicals we sent them as listed in the Riegle Report.

The list was growing of possible reasons for health problems of the Gulf War Veterans. Was it chemical exposure, PB tablets, Anthrax vaccine? All I knew was I was sick along with 250,000 other Veterans. I received a second letter regarding Khamisiyah in 2005.

The following letter dated 9-27-2005, states basically the death rates among service members exposed to the Khamisiyah demolition remain the same with only a higher rate of those dying from brain cancer!

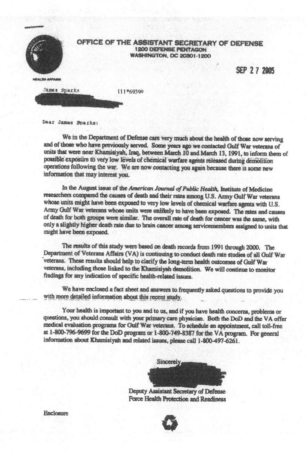

2001 I was still waiting to hear something on my appeal. I continued working, pushing through each day but struggling physically on a daily basis. Driving home one evening from a friend's house I was rear-ended by a drunk driver. Our vehicle was totaled and I spent the next 12 months under chiropractic care for my back injury.

I continued to push through. My body was sending all kinds of signals: skin rash was still there, fatigue, migraines, back pain, leg pain, numbness and tingling in my hands and arms. I just remembered; I did see another civilian Doctor a Dermatologist. I had those spots on the calves of my legs checked out. He diagnosed it as "Morphea," another rare skin condition, autoimmune disease. The lumps on the trunk of my body were diagnosed as "lipoma's" benign tumors. I kept pushing through. I had to travel out of state for my job. I was driving a blazer with stick shift on the floor. My left foot wouldn't work; my leg was numb. What now? I managed somehow.

August 16, 2002, I received a decision letter regarding my appeal from the 1998 decision. DENIED and 27 pages long. I appealed the decision within a few days of receiving their letter. I am pissed off having gathered so much research, went to all the requested Dr, appts, even became a Guinea pig again for the Gov. participating in their Mycoplasma study, only to be let down again with no answers to my failing health! I requested copies of all my records from the regional office and came across the following:

It's called CAPS notes from a rater at the VA regional office below: I will summarize. It was a validation for us regarding my complaints of numbness and tingling bilateral in both arms. The person who reviewed my records noticed an error he quoted the following law, "rating decision overlooked 38 CFR 3.317(a)(1)(ii) and goes on to say carpal tunnel was ruled out. That was a win for me and I used their own law to appeal the decision.

PRINTED FROM CAPS
AU NOTES: 03-17-00
3/17/2000 3:21 PM; VSCMCATA

The veteran's County Veterans Service Officer (CVSO) brought the VA's letter of 03-03-00 (see above) to the attention of Frank Bongiovanni requesting clarification as to what evidence the veteran needed to submit.

The veteran is already service connected for: dysthymic disorder with anxiety (which includes his complaints of chronic fatigue and anti-social behavior); lipoma, thigh and left rib area (which includes the morphea); and seborrheic dermatitis. The veteran's CVSO was informed that the veteran will be scheduled for VA examination for these conditions 60 days from 03-03-00 in order to allow the veteran time to submit additional evidence to support his new claims for sleep trouble and back problems due to undiagnosed illness. The veteran's CVSO was also informed that the veteran's sleeping problems were used in the evaluation of his dysthymic disorder with anxiety and that if he wanted to claim his sleeping problems as a separate disability he should notify VA and provide evidence showing that his sleeping problems are of unknown etiology. In terms of the veteran's back condition, the CVSO was informed that the veteran should also submit evidence showing that his back condition is chronic and is of unknown etiology. The veteran's current medical records from VAMC Dayton (which have been requested) should be reviewed in light of his new claimed conditions prior to scheduling VA examination.

The veteran's CVSO was also informed that the veteran's bilateral numbness and tingling of the arms would also be examined. The letter of 03-03-00 informed the veteran that we needed new and material evidence to reopen his claim for bilateral numbness and tingling of the arms. However, further review of the C-file shows that the veteran was denied for this condition by rating decision of 03-24-98 because there were no signs of bilateral numbness and tingling of the arms in-service nor any in other medical evidence reviewed at that time. It appears that this rating decision overlooked 38 CFR 3.317(a)(1)(ii) which provides that a veteran may be compensated for certain disabilities due to undiagnosed illness if they became manifest while in service or to a degree of 10% or more no later that 12-31-01; and cannot be attributed to any know clinical diagnoses. The veteran's latest VA examination (dated July/August 1997 and cited in the aforementioned rating decision) showed an impression of "intermittent sensory phenomena of uncertain etiology" as to the veteran's bilateral numbness and tingling of the arms. Carpal tunnel syndrome was ruled out. In addition, the symptoms described by the veteran may entitled him to a 10% evaluation.

The veteran's CVSO also inquired as to our statement in the 03-03-00 letter to the veteran stating that the lab results he submitted (done in connection with a VA study of the correlation between Mycoplasma Fermentans and Gulf War illness) showed the veteran with Mycoplasma Genitalium. This statement was included in the 03-03-00 letter IN ERROR as it was intended a note for CAPS only. The CVSO was informed that the lab report was a clinical finding and not a diagnosis and could not be used (by itself) to grant compensation.

March 1, 2003 After receiving their CAP notes, I submitted another appeal using their notes and regulation that they quoted!

December 15, 2003, we received another decision. My case was remanded. A victory! My 1998 case was still alive! It's eleven pages long. I won't bore you with it; it's full of regulations, but this time in my favor! It even mentions that old Veteran civilian doctor. I saw his medical notes helped my case! We received a letter to appear in front of the Board. We were going to Cleveland to the VA Regional Office. Finally, we would meet the OZ behind the curtain?

I scheduled an appointment with the local VA rep. to discuss my case before going in front of the Board. She wasn't as optimistic. She said, "You don't have any new medical evidence to add, so there's no point in going! "She went on to say, "You should just claim the 'mental'; try and increase the rating you have."

I was furious. I proceeded to tell her, "It's not just about me. Something happened to all of us over there. It's not about the money. I want to know what is wrong with me--with all of us." I walked out leaving Melissa sitting there.

She tells me the Rep asked if I was coming back. Melissa said, "Yes."

Melissa told me on the ride home that the VA rep said, "They (the Regional office) find it hard to believe he is disabled because of the letters he writes."

Melissa told her, "He's sick not stupid!"

I had made my decision to go to Cleveland. I needed to go -- after ten years of fighting, writing letters and numerous doctor appointments. We drove 3 hours one way to Cleveland only to find parking was going to be a problem, parking meters with one-hour time limits. We had no idea how long we would be in the Government building. We dropped the coins in the parking meter and headed into the building not knowing what to expect. We went through a metal detector and took the elevator. We were greeted and asked to have a seat. It wasn't long and a tall gentleman came and got us. We followed him to a small room. Jim and I both looked at each other; the room was like a broom closet with a small desk, two chairs and a fan oscillating behind our head. The man asked permission to record our conversation. I told him my story. We didn't bring any documentation. We told him they have everything, all medical records and my research on Gulf War Illness. I needed to tell them my symptoms face-to-face after all the years of writing appeals, from the very first claim in 1993. He didn't offer much feedback; he listened without much interruption. He said they would make a decision soon and as usual I would receive a letter in the mail. We left feeling satisfied and happy to see the old blazer didn't get towed. By now, I had been battling the VA for 10 years. I managed to keep my claim alive with multiple appeals.

2004 We were back to our routine, me feeling my health decline trying to hide most of it from Melissa and the girls. She wasn't fooled. I was waking up most nights, my arms numb and tingling. The migraines would come with a vengeance. The stabbing ice pick feeling in my eye would render me immobile. I couldn't lie down. I couldn't hide this from the girls. They knew when I had them to stay clear. There was nothing anyone could do. I would eat Advil trying to get some relief. Life should have been great. Melissa was doing well at her job. I was an Engineer and the girls were now teenagers, running track and competing on the swim team. I was struggling, questioning why I couldn't keep up with my peers. I questioned if I was crazy. Were these symptoms all in my head as the VA had me believe?

In June 2004, I walked off the job. I couldn't do it any more along with all my other symptoms. I was now experiencing dizziness and complete exhaustion. I was already home when Melissa got home from work. I told her I quit my job; somebody was going to get hurt. I didn't tell her that day of my new symptoms just that I couldn't do it anymore. She didn't say much. I knew she would worry. I was the breadwinner. We wouldn't last long financially without me working. I told her I had faith and she should too.

I stayed home trying to recover. Life went on. The girls went to school and Melissa went to work.

November 18, 2004, I stumbled around the house most of the day. Literally stumbling, my right side felt funny, and my fingers felt puffy. I tried writing and I couldn't. Was I crazy? What was happening to me? Melissa came home from work and I told her how I was feeling. She didn't hesitate and said we were going to the emergency room. So, we drove the forty-five-minute drive to the Dayton VA. During the initial intake at the emergency room, the nurse expressed concern of a stroke based on my symptoms. She commented on my speech and noticed it was slurred. We all said no that's not new. Looking back, I realized we were all used to this symptom; my speech would be slurred, some days better than others. We tried to explain my health problems and told them I was stumbling, my hands and fingers were puffy, I couldn't write my name, and that I hadn't been sleeping, but I was exhausted. They had me write my name and looked at me like I was crazy when I managed to scribble my name. I was told there was not a neurologist available and they would have to make me an appointment. They prescribed me sleeping pills and sent me home. Below are the VA emergency room doctor's notes. Again, they blame my symptoms on psychosomatic (meaning my physical symptoms were caused by or aggravated by a mental factor such as stress!) Thirteen years later and they are still telling me it's all in my head, and still no MRI.

Below is the VA Er visit notes: after sending me home with sleeping pills they also state "the patient requests an MRI, states he wants to know what happen to him in Gulf War," They spelled Gulf as golf, really, and goes on to say he seems to be preoccupied with his claim and feels very frustrated.

We arrived home and I think all of us were in shock. Another day and no answers. I threw the sleeping pills away. Melissa was begging me to go to the civilian ER. I didn't want to go. Not that I didn't want answers but I didn't want to burden the family with debt. We were already struggling financially wondering if we would have to file bankruptcy. I had been out of work for five months. We didn't have health insurance and how would we pay for an ER visit? I tried to reassure Melissa that I would be okay and to have faith!

November 23, 2004 I couldn't take it any longer. I was bouncing off the walls, literally. Our youngest daughter Jennifer came home from school and I said you have to take me to the hospital, and you have to drive. She knew instantly something was seriously wrong: first that I wanted to go to the emergency room, and second that I wanted her to drive. She was 16 and had not had her license long. She called her mother at work and told her what was going on, and said meet us there. This time we went to a civilian hospital emergency room. They did the usual tests and weren't too sure what was going on. Melissa asked about an MRI. They stated they couldn't do one until the morning but would admit me and do it first thing. We all agreed! I was admitted: Melissa and the girls went home. By the time she returned in the morning, they had already completed an MRI of the brain. Within a short amount of time the doctor was in the room to tell us I had Multiple Sclerosis. That I was having an exacerbation with multiple active lesions. Also based on my medical history and the number of old lesions I had had it for a long time!

Melissa and the girls were crying. I, on the other hand, was almost elated. At least I had a diagnosis. I wasn't crazy; although, it was in my head! They started me on IV steroids immediately and began to talk about how important it was that I start on a disease modifying drug? Within a short amount of time, I was pretty pumped up on steroids. My mind was racing. I told Melissa to contact the local Veterans rep that we had been working with. The neurologist team picked up on my anxiety and I began to tell him my story of how I had begged the VA for years to do an MRI, how I had been sick for thirteen years, and they had me believe I was crazy. I didn't turn to drugs or alcohol like so many, which I don't blame them. I kept fighting and having faith that I would find answers. He said I have someone you need to speak with. It was his partner. She was a neurologist that just so happened to work part time at the Dayton VA.

She came in the next day and explained she reviewed my medical records and she went on to say you are one of the ones that should have been seen by a neurologist at the VA. I explained to her that I had been in fact seen by a neurologist at the VA and they didn't help me or listen to me. I explained that my VA claim was on appeal and that they needed this information. She agreed to thoroughly review my VA medical records and would render a decision.

I spent the next seven days in the hospital receiving IV steroids. You talk about a "high." I was there. The doctor told myself and Melissa that if I began to hallucinate to let them know. By day six I was on the verge. The Neurologist that happened to work part-time at the Dayton VA came in and said "I reviewed all your VA medical records and I have no doubt based on your VA medical records and your MRI that you have had MS since 1991!" BOOM!

I asked her if she would write up what she found? She agreed. I called my VA rep. and told her proof was coming for my claim.

Below is a nexus letter. That's what the VA calls proof from a DOCTOR She basically states "there is no doubt he has had symptoms since 1991 based on health history and his MRI results. Also, <u>he has been truthful and consistent with his complaints!</u>"

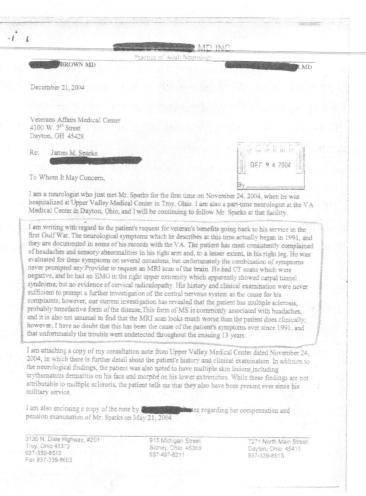

Page 2
James M. Sparks

As stated above, this was one of several examinations at the VA that addressed the patient's complaints and yet did not fully zero-in on the cause of the symptoms; however, I have gone over this note with Ms. Adams-Cortez and I have underlined a few points that we feel are important for Mr. Sparks. Specifically, he has complained of headache beginning even prior to this discharge in 1991. It is also important to note that at least the patient's complaints have been fully consistent every time that he is seen at the VA. This fact would speak to the authenticity of his complaints and the likelihood that they do indeed go all the way back to his military service.

Finally, I am enclosing a copy of Mr. Sparks' MRI report which documents his diagnosis. If I can offer any further information, please do not hesitate to contact me. My private office telephone number is (937)▓▓▓▓▓▓▓and I can be reached at the VA at (937)▓▓▓▓▓▓

Thank you for your attention to and reconsideration of Mr. Sparks' application for veteran's benefits.

Sincerely yours,

▓▓▓▓▓▓rown, MD

esb/llm

Enclosures

The next two pages are the civilian doctor's notes who also worked part time at the VA. In summary she states through all this time no one ever requested a brain MRI!

CONSULTATION   SPARKS, JAMES M - 002-575

was psychological.

He has also continued to have significant right retroorbital headache for several weeks or months now. The headache seems to come every evening and night. He notes at some point he was treated with amitriptyline, which did not help. He does not know if he has taken any other preventive medications. The only things that he has been taking recently have been Advil or Tylenol as needed for headache. He is on no prescription medications.

Through all of this time, no one has ever requested a MRI scan of the brain. When the patient did not improve after his recent visit to the VA Hospital, he decided to seek treatment here at Upper Valley Medical Center. Because his speech seemed mildly slurred and his gait unsteady, he was admitted for further evaluation and treatment. CT scan of the brain in the emergency department was normal except for evidence of mild sinusitis in the maxillary and ethmoid sinuses.

The patient denies any recent problems with cough, shortness of breath, chest pain, or palpitations. He sometimes get nausea with bad headaches, but has no vomiting. There is no other difficulty with nausea, diarrhea, or constipation. When questioned about bladder control, he says that he has never been incontinent. However, sometimes he has difficulty starting his stream. He also has occasional urgency.

The patient has never had any loss of vision or double vision.

NEUROLOGICAL EXAMINATION
GENERAL APPEARANCE: The patient is a well-developed, well-nourished, 40-year-old, white male in no acute distress. He is alert and fully oriented and has no memory or language deficits. However, there is mild dysarthria.
VITAL SIGNS: Blood pressure 116/75, pulse 94 and regular, respirations 20 and unlabored. He is afebrile.
SKIN: He has an erythematous scaly rash on the face and arms, and to a lesser extent on the legs. There are also oval areas of hyperpigmentation on each lateral calf. He says that these are the areas of morphea, which are now much less intense than they used to be.
CRANIAL NERVE: Visual fields full to confrontation. Pupils are equal, round, and reactive to light. There is no afferent pupillary defect. Eye movements are full and conjugate and without nystagmus. There is no ptosis. Facial sensation is equal bilaterally. There is some flattening of the right nasal labial fold and slight right facial weakness when he smiles. Otherwise, the face moves well bilaterally. The gag reflex is normal. The tongue protrudes slightly to the right side.
NECK: Supple. Carotid pulses are 2+ bilaterally and without bruits.
MOTOR: No involuntary movements. There is a mild pronation drift of the right upper extremity. No atrophy or fasciculations are seen. On manual muscle testing, strength is 5/5 in all muscle groups. Deep tendon reflexes are hyperactive throughout, even more so on the right than the left, with a few beats of ankle clonus on the right side. Plantar responses flexor on the left and equivocal on the right. The gait

Printed by:
Printed on: Page 2 of 4

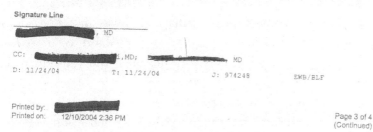

CONSULTATION   SPARKS, JAMES M - 002-575

shows some clumsiness and possible circumduction of the right lower extremity when he walks. He is able to walk on his heels and on his toes but has trouble with tandem.

SENSORY: Sensory testing is within normal limits bilaterally.

CEREBELLAR: Cerebellar examination shows no dysmetria on finger-nose-finger testing with either hand. There is no truncal ataxia.

LABORATORY DATA

MRI scan of the brain shows multiple lesions of varying sizes in the subcortical and periventricular white matter of the brain. Some of the periventricular lesions are oval in shape and perpendicular to the ventricles. A few of the lesions are quite large, but there is no surrounding edema. The lesions do enhance with contrast.

The patient's CBC is normal except for a white count of 13.3. Comprehensive metabolic profile is unremarkable, as are thyroid levels. Urine drug screen is clear. Urinalysis is normal.

IMPRESSION

The MRI scan is virtually diagnostic for multiple sclerosis. Not mentioned above is the fact that the patient also has a lesion in the corpus callosum. The radiologist has interpreted this as a tumefactive form of multiple sclerosis (MS), which classically looks severe on MRI scan but yields mild findings on clinical examination. I believe that MS would explain all of the patient's neurological symptoms and fatigue since 1991.

The headaches may or may not be a part of the current syndrome of demyelinating disease. This may be a separate issue with migraine.

RECOMMENDATIONS

1. I agree with lumbar puncture.
2. High-dose intravenous Solu-Medrol.
3. I would treat the headaches symptomatically for now. If they do not resolve with steroid treatment, then we could start working with prophylactic medication.
4. Once the patient is stable, we should start him on interferon therapy.

Thank you for this consultation.

Signature Line

_____ , MD

CC: _____ , MD; _____ , MD

D: 11/24/04   T: 11/24/04   J: 974248   EWB/BLF

Printed by: _____
Printed on: 12/10/2004 2:36 PM

Page 3 of 4
(Continued)

I left the hospital with a list of prescriptions and a notice that a nurse would be coming to my home to explain how I needed to inject myself every other day with an immunotherapy drug to try and stop my own immune system from attacking my brain. There is no cure only medicine to try and stop your immune system from attacking your brain. The only treatment then and currently when you're having an exacerbation is IV steroids.

Reluctantly, again having no health insurance (the injections alone were eleven hundreds each) and facing bankruptcy once again, I scheduled a follow-up appointment with the VA. Melissa asked to speak with a patient advocate to begin to try and express our frustration with the care or I should say lack of care that I had received from the Dayton VA hospital. She listened and seemed concerned but not much changed. I was scheduled with the same neurologist that I had been seeing and who refused to give me an MRI. Upon explaining my recent diagnosis with him, he seemed to dismiss my diagnosis and wanted to discuss his previous diagnosis of carpal tunnel syndrome regarding the numbness and tingling I had in my arms and hands. I explained to him that I did not want his surgery and that the civilian doctors believed the brain damage (brain lesions) were causing my symptoms.

He was a tall, skinny, backwards kinda' guy. He became defensive and threatened to call a patient advocate. I agreed!

The only thing that came from that meeting was I was assigned to a new neurologist. She was okay and managed my meds that were prescribed from the civilian neurologist team. The Dayton VA did add a new prescription. As I had previously tried to explain to another one of their neurologists, I was having trouble urinating. It was another symptom the VA doctors chose to ignore. As a man it was hard to admit or let my wife see that I had to sit down on the toilet to try and urinate. I would feel the urge to go but the stream would not start. I would try everything, running water and pushing on my bladder. The Dayton VA finally addressed this issue and prescribed a prescription to help. It didn't help. I found out years later it was the wrong script! Another F up by the VA. The script I later learned was for overactive bladders!

I spent the next two years trying to adjust to my new normal. I won that 1995 appeal in 2005. Well not totally, the VA got me here: As you will see below, they acknowledge in 1998 that I didn't get their decision letter in 1996 from the 1995 claim. Confusing right? Imagine being sick and trying to fight the red tape, never being able to talk to a human, only being able to dispute their ignorance by letters. To this day, I don't know how many appeals I submitted. I'm too tired to count, but I know it was numerous!

I did finally receive after thirteen years of fighting and searching for answers to my health problems a rating decision in my favor in 2005 with a retroactive date to the VA's logic of 1999. I did appeal again trying to get them to recognize it should have been retroactive to 1995, but I lost. By now I was exhausted from fighting the system and all the red tape. They won that battle.

The back pay we received pulled us from the ever-looming cliff of bankruptcy that we were sure we were facing. We were grateful.

I received a few more letters from the VA stating I was rated ninety percent and unemployable. I eventually fought that and was awarded hundred percent permanently and totally disabled. This offered some benefits to my family. By now my oldest daughter had graduated high school and was going to college. The VA helped cover this cost. She also gave us a hope for the future, a grandson Kaleb James! She became an LPN. I had a lot of time on my hands. I spent a lot of that time researching what happened to us. I began to dig deeper into the Anthrax vaccine we received in the desert. There is a lot of research and information out there now about this controversial vaccine. I will attempt to summarize what I have learned and why I believe I had an adverse reaction to the Anthrax vaccine!

First, I will offer a little history; the anthrax vaccine was licensed in 1970 for manufacture by the Michigan Dept. of Public Health. The plant and product line were sold to a private company BioPort, located in Lansing, Michigan, the only US manufacturer as of 2002 to manufacture the vaccine. After the initial dose you would need additional doses administered weeks then months apart with a final booster (for a total of six). The vaccine according to (Army Information Paper,1991) was given to more than 150,000 service members during Operation Desert Storm 1991. In 1998 it was decided by the Secretary of Defense to vaccinate all US service members against anthrax, increasing the number vaccinated to 522,529 service members as of 2001. (Institute of Medicine (US) Committee to Assess the safety of the Anthrax Vaccine: Joellenbeck

LM, Zwanziger LL, Durch JS, et al..editors. The Anthrax Vaccine: Is it safe? Does it Work? Washington (DC): National Academies Press (US);2002 2, Background)

From what I can gather now the company sold and is operating under Emergent BioDefense Operations Inc. in Lansing, Michigan. According to the FDA the "Next-generation anthrax vaccines are under development by multiple manufactures." It's easy to get in the weeds regarding the risk of the Anthrax vaccine. So, I will do my best to summarize: Our Government, as of the 70's had a stockpile of anthrax vaccine, but it required a series of six inoculations over 12 to 18 months. Going to war, knowing we had sold them anthrax as a bioweapon, our government knew they had to protect us from the risk. One theory is they modified the anthrax vaccine using an adjuvant, such as squalene. It is a "naturally occurring substance found in shark liver oil, some vegetable oils, and in the human liver. It can also be manufactured through chemical engineering, "By adding this it is intended to enhance and optimize the immune responses to vaccines." Not to over simplify but the theory is because it is naturally occurring, the body ignores this and loses its ability to distinguish what is normal from what is foreign. When tolerance is broken the immune system turns on itself attacking the body it is supposed to defend. Studies regarding this go back to the 1950's. Results of that time showed animals injected with the adjuvant developed terrible conditions such as encephalomyelitis, Multiple sclerosis, inflammation, allergic reaction to name a few. I began to research the manufacturer of the Anthrax vaccine BioPort. I contacted them and received the following letter:

So basically this letter from Bio-Port, makers of the Anthrax vaccine, acknowledges my symptoms match their adverse reaction to the vaccine!

CORPORATION   3500 N. Martin Luther King Jr. Blvd. • Lansing, Michigan 48906

September 26, 2005

Mr. James Sparks

Dear James:

BioPort Corporation has reviewed your submission to the Food and Drug Administration (FDA) in connection with Docket No. 1980N-0208. In your submission, you indicated that it is your belief that you, or a close associate(s), may have been harmed by anthrax vaccine adsorbed.

We have reviewed prior VAERS submissions and discovered a match based on the adverse event information you provided. If you have additional clinical information concerning an adverse event reported previously to VAERS, you may provide this new information to VAERS by updating the enclosed VAERS form, on which you should indicate your previously assigned VAERS number in the top right-hand corner and check "follow-up" in box # 27 of the form. Alternatively, you can contact VAERS at 1-800-822-7967 or by visiting www.vaers.hhs.gov. The Medical Affairs Department at BioPort is available at 1-877-246-8472 to assist you in the completion of this form.

Yours truly,

Vice President, Medical Affairs

I also learned of the (VAERS) system, Vaccine Adverse Event Reporting System. It is listed as a national vaccine safety surveillance program co-sponsored by the FDA. Who Knew? Even today most people let alone Veterans are familiar with this data-base. Their letter states the adverse reaction I reported matches one of the risks or adverse reactions individuals can have after receiving the vaccine. Multiple sclerosis! I also submitted a letter to the FDA regarding what I felt was an adverse reaction to the Anthrax vaccine: below. However, they even admit that having not used the anthrax vaccine widely, there are no long-term studies on the adverse reaction to the vaccine.

In 1998 the Clinton Administration required the inoculation of all military members with the Anthrax vaccine. In June 2001, I think even in 2000 the DOD stopped vaccinations due to non- FDA approved changes in Bio Ports manufacturing process. But it wasn't long before the mandatory inoculation began again. To my knowledge it continues today.

The letter below is what I wrote and submitted to the FDA regarding the risk and adverse health effects from the Anthrax vaccine.

12/27/16, 11:30 AM

1980N-0208 - Biological Products; Bacterial Vaccines and Toxoids; Implementation of Efficacy Review
FDA Comment Number :   EC29

Submitter : Mr. James Sparks   Date & Time: 03/01/2005 07:03:00

Organization : Mr. James Sparks

                Individual Consumer

Category :

Issue Areas/Comments

GENERAL

GENERAL

20 January 1991, during Desert Storm, under orders, our company was injected with a single dose 'SECRET' Anthrax vaccine. This vaccine likely contained Squalene, an oil adjuvant, illegal in the United States for human use.
The 1970 FDA approved anthrax vaccine requires six injections at precise intervals to be effective but it was still ineffective against many strains of anthrax.
The FDA has tested and found Squalene in incremental doses in various Anthrax Vaccine lots dating back to Desert Storm, suggesting research using doubling doses to test human tolerance to Squalene.
Squalene is known to induce Multiple Sclerosis. Adjuvants also are known to induce Scleroderma. I developed Scleroderma and Multiple Sclerosis since the Anthrax Vaccine. I feel I have other underlying yet undiagnosed autoimmune diseases as well. I feel my entire body is affected with autoimmune disease as a result of Squalene laced Anthrax Vaccine injection.
BioPort disclosed ON January 31, 2002, the date on the new product insert, that recipients of anthrax vaccine reported allergic reactions and autoimmune disease as a consequence of anthrax vaccination. The product insert lists the following serious adverse events as infrequently reported by recipients of anthrax vaccine: pemphigus vulgaris, endocarditis, angioderma and other hypersensitivity reactions, idiopathic thrombocytopenia purpura, collagen vascular disease, systemic lupus erythematosus, multiple sclerosis, polyarteritis, inflammatory arthritis, transverse myelitis and glomerulonephritis. All are dysfunctions of the immune system or diseases that are specifically autoimmune. Other infrequently reported events include cellulitis, cysts, pemphigus vulgaris, endocarditis, sepsis, angioedema and other hypersensitivity reactions. The VA refuses to test for antibodies to Squalene, or fund this testing that is available. While Walter Reed has created its own antibodies to Squalene assay and filed for patent of their antibodies to Squalene assay.

This SECRET Anthrax Vaccine broke my immune tolerance, inducing multiple Lipoma within 60-90 days, Scleroderma within six months to one year, and Multiple Sclerosis symptoms within one year. I have no doubt this Multiple Sclerosis involves my brain and spinal cord, causing inflammation of my peripheral nervous system and this has evolved into irreversible central nervous system damage and chronic pain.

The VA, in their refusal to perform advanced testing has left this diagnosis to remain hidden, untreated, and prolonged personal suffering. This has violated everything I ever imagined to be American values. These past 14 years, behind my eyes, has been nothing less than torture. I suspect, as many others do, that the VA diagnostic protocol is skewed to dismiss early stages of autoimmune diseases, thus leaving everyone scratching their heads and declaring Gulf War Syndrome for so long.

I also suspect (as many others) that there is an abundance of yet undiagnosed autoimmune disease within Desert Storm and Operation Iraqi Freedom Veterans. I also understand the risk vs. benefit argument the DoD presents as well as plans to use the Anthrax Vaccine in the civilian population if needed. These arguments become moot when those responsible refuse to admit any flaws or errors in their judgments and decisions. For too long, many have needlessly suffered so a few can keep a filthy secret for monetary gain.

The Anthrax vaccine insert that I have can no longer be found on the web. It lists again among many ailments, specifically, autoimmune diseases that it can cause. During this time, I also came across the book *Vaccine-A* written by Gary Matsumoto. He writes about how the Army had been working on a new Anthrax vaccine. I recommend this book. As with most things today, you can search the web and find arguments on either side of this controversy. Tulane University Medical Center School of Medicine, with Robert Garry leading the research found that sick Gulf War soldiers were found to have squalene antibodies in their blood. Although to this day the government spends thousands of dollars for research into the Gulf War illness, the Pentagon disagreed with a GAO report that recommends the Secretary of Defense should test for antibodies to squalene in the blood of sick Gulf War veterans. I continued, when I could, to research this and follow Gulf War web-sites.

Life went on Melissa was still working and our youngest turned 18 and moved out on her own. I putted around the house taking my injections every other day. Melissa became concerned that I was depressed. I was on the most medication I had ever taken. My pain level was still high and I was trying to adjust to a world where I wasn't working. My migraines were coming with a vengeance and the doctors tried managing them with different prescriptions.

2007 My vision was changing. It felt as if I was looking through a tunnel and colors were not as bright. Having the internet at my fingertips now, I read about optic neuritis. It is pretty common in people who have a demyelinating disease of the brain. We scheduled an appointment with the VA and confirmed this diagnosis. Their answer was more steroids. The last experience of IV steroids had me pretty hyped up and not sleeping for days.

The optic neuritis eventually passed and I recovered most of my vision. Life sometimes felt it was passing me by. Melissa with my encouragement enrolled in college. Between her work schedule and college classes, she was gone a lot. The kids were growing up and starting their own lives

2009 I finally found an attorney who would take my case to sue the United States of America for medical malpractice; this would be a tort claim. I believed it was medical malpractice after begging the Dayton VA for 13 years to help me, to even just give me an MRI …to no avail. However; if you have ever tried to sue any doctor or hospital, you know they stick together. My attorney advised me that my case would be difficult to win in court because Multiple Sclerosis was difficult to diagnose.

The attorneys called and said they couldn't find a neurologist to testify in court. My neurologists said that had I been diagnosed sooner and put on these drugs, there would be a change in the severity of the damage already done to my brain.

Melissa and I wouldn't fully understand the extent of this damage until later. Upon advice of our attorney, I settled the claim in 2010. We received a small monetary amount.

In 2011, I woke up only to find I couldn't walk! What was happening now? With the urging of Melissa, I once again found myself at the hospital, a civilian hospital. I again had active brain lesions and required IV steroids to stop the progression. I spent a week in the hospital. Melissa was by my side every day.

2012, I suffered another attack; my immune system was attacking my brain. I refused to go to the hospital. Knowing my history, the VA authorized a nurse to come into the home to provide another round of IV steroids. The nurse came in daily and slowly I regained my ability to walk again. Although not a hundred percent, I walked a little slower.

I have asked my loving wife of 36 years to help tell my story, our story. My injury has left me with short-term memory loss and difficulty focusing so with this I'll leave you with her and with the help of my journals and research, she will carry-on!

2013, I *"Melissa"* was at the peak of my career but we were struggling. I was worried about Jim, rightfully so. His health was declining and each attack brought on new or worsening of his symptoms. The winters were harder on him; he had fallen more times than I can count. For the most part he sat at home. On a good day he managed to go golfing or hunting. But those days were far and few between. I sat him down and said, "Look, my boss is talking about retiring and I'm pretty much guaranteed a promotion. But I don't want to take it because it will be longer hours and require me to travel more. I want us to move to Florida." I loved my career and the people I worked with were like family to me. But, I knew my husband was not well. His brother and our youngest daughter already resided there so we knew the area, somewhat. I had hatched the plan and put it in motion. Before he knew it, we were selling our home and moving to Florida. Our oldest daughter actually bought the home they had come to know as the homestead. We liquidated and were able to buy a nice older home in Florida on the Gulf side. I found a job. We spent a lot of time sightseeing and enjoying our new home.

To this day, Jim struggles with our decision to move to Florida. Not that he doesn't like Florida, he just has no memory of why we made the decision. I didn't understand how sick he was, how much he was struggling mentally. The local VA in Ohio gave us no clue about the mind storm Jim was enduring and what the future could hold.

Once again, I was concerned and new things weren't right with Jim. We went through the process of getting established at a new VA hospital. Right off the bat the new prime care doctor was adamant about changing his prescriptions that he now had been on since being diagnosed in November 2004. His new neurologist also wanted to change his injections from every other day to a new drug that just hit the market that was a pill you could take daily. I wasn't totally against change but as usual it's the way the prime care doctor handled it.

At one of his scheduled appointments with his prime care doctor, I was trying to tell her that he wasn't sleeping and had been losing weight for some time now. He was probably down to 175 from an average of 210 lbs. The doctor actually reached over, patted his knee and said to him are you drinking while she's at work? What the hell? I thought I was going to come unglued. We let her know that he did not drink. She stopped his pain meds, and prescribed two new drugs, baclofen and tramadol. Again, maybe it was not so bad to change meds but she stopped his meds abruptly, no weening off at all! Add to that he started the new MS drug Tecfidera. Jim and I were both noticing even before moving to Florida that things were not only changing physically for him but mentally too. He struggled with completing tasks or trying to just get things together to leave the house. He was always losing his wallet, keys, you name it. He always had me looking for something.

Once he was established with his prime care doctor, he was assigned a neurologist, he wasn't too sure about him. He was from New York, pretty direct and to the point. That, Jim did like. One of his first appointments with him he said, "I probably shouldn't say this but the radiologist and I have looked at your MRI's, and we have no idea how you're still walking or functioning at your current level."

One of the things he did was schedule Jim to be seen by a neuropsychologist. The initial appointment was a lengthy test, including things like problem solving and memory tests to name a few things. The test is done to assess the severity of cognitive dysfunction. Jim left that appointment feeling defeated. He drove directly to my job and called me from the truck. He couldn't go into my office. I came out and he began to cry. I think that assessment was a validation to Jim that his mind was not what it used to be. He was always an overachiever and tried to succeed at everything he did. He struggled with this assessment. I cried as he explained, "he didn't feel he did well on the assessment." The feeling was not like failing an exam but a realization his mind was not functioning as it should. A few weeks later we had a follow-up appointment to get the results of the neuro assessment.

They began to explain that his brain was like a computer and the processor was running slow. I asked about his memory issues. "Is it like Alzheimer's?"

"No," the doctor began to explain, "his memories are there but the path to retrieve them is damaged and they may come to him, slowly or with some assistance." They went on to say,

"We don't recommend he drive anymore. His ability to process things around him are affected." Another validation for both Jim and I! He had experienced a few close calls while driving. He even had trouble with directions.

Why had no one told us he could face cognitive deficit? I had often argued with the doctors about letting me sit in on appointments because he was struggling with his short-term memory.

So here we were in beautiful Florida. Once again, he was withdrawing and sitting at home while I was at work. I was concerned; I noticed things he didn't recognize. For example, he was making bad financial decisions. Salesmen (door knockers) in Florida are abundant! I also noticed he was becoming paranoid thinking the worst of anyone and everyone. He still wasn't sleeping much and still losing weight even though he hadn't changed his eating habits. Along with his physical decline, for example trouble walking his walking pace was that of an eighty-year-old who was not in good shape.

October 1, 2014 Unbeknownst to Jim, I was reaching out to the VA seeking help. I worried every day when I had to leave him to go to work. I reached a social worker at the Bay Pines VA hospital. where he had now been receiving his medical care and expressed my concerns about his behavior and struggles with activities of daily living. To my amazement the social worker was very receptive and scheduled an in-home assessment within a week. The VA never moved this fast. I was in shock! An appointment was scheduled. The gentlemen that contacted me explained that Jim had been approved for in-home health care and that if I wanted, I could quit my job and be his caregiver. I came home from work and began to tell Jim about the conversation. He didn't understand at the time, but he didn't fight it. The gentleman came and met with us; I signed some papers and told Jim I was quitting my job to stay home and be with him. This was around the first of October 2014.

October 21, 2014

I was feeling pretty good. I no longer had to worry about working. I could stay home and care for my husband. I thought no one could or would do a better job of looking after him than me. We had now been married for 31 years. I had dreams of taking him to the beach, museums, and traveling. You name it; we could do it. October 21, 2014, changed us both forever. Jim and I were sitting on the couch getting ready to go over some paperwork. It was a beautiful morning in Florida. The sun was shining and it was warm and a little breeze in the air. Jim didn't sleep the night before. Jim was quiet as we began to go over some paperwork; his legs were jerking. I looked at him and said, "Jim, are you ok?" He didn't answer. Sensing something wasn't right, I jumped up and stood in front of him. He was just staring straight ahead. I called his name again and he didn't answer. I called 911, and I told the operator something was wrong with my husband as he was just staring at me. I said, "Jim, say my name!" I'm not sure why I asked that; I guess looking back, it was something simple that he should be able to do. He said, "Melissa," and began to have a grand mal seizure!

Having never witnessed someone having a seizure, I was terrified. I pleaded with the 911 operator to hurry and send someone.

They were asking me questions I wasn't sure I could answer. "Was he breathing?"

I said, "Yes." His head was turned to the left; his eyes were open, his legs straight out and his whole body was jerking.

It felt like an eternity. My instinct was to stay with him and reassure him. I didn't know if he could hear me, but I kept telling him I was here and that an ambulance was on the way. They finally arrived. They came in and scooped him up from our couch like you would pick up an infant. They cradled him and carried him to the stretcher. They could see I was distraught, and told me I should ride with them. I could hear them say. "He's having another one as I climbed into the ambulance." Our youngest daughter Jennifer was living in Florida. I managed to call her to let her know we were headed to the hospital. We arrived at the closest ER. They swooped Jim away and then came for me. I told them what medicines he was on and the doctor began telling me they wanted to give him a drug that could be dangerous but they recommend it. They had done a CT scan of his brain, and at this point, they weren't sure what was going on. Our daughter arrived and we agreed to give him the drug. They called me over and Jim was lying in the hospital bed, his right arm was up in the air. He couldn't put it down. He had wet himself and was lying there in a fetal position quietly. All I could think to say was everything is going to be okay. Still not knowing what happened or why.

They admitted Jim to the hospital. By the time they got him to his room, he was coming around. It was now in the evening. He had been without his normal meds. He became angry and wanted to go home. The doctor came in and Jim was convinced that he was okay and wanted to go home. The doctor was not very helpful from my perspective. She didn't explain what he just went through, that he should stay, or offer any medicine to help calm him down. He checked out "AMA" (against medical advice)!

We had contacted our daughter Jessica who was living in Ohio. She booked the next flight to Florida and arrived first thing the next morning. That was a blessing. She was an LPN and wasn't happy about him checking out from the hospital. She called his neurologist at the VA and explained what had happened. The neurologist was very concerned and advised that Jim should come to the ER because he could have another seizure.

Upon waking the next morning, Jim seemed okay. He was quiet, but okay until he began to drink his coffee, and he choked. Jessica explained that she had spoken to his doctor and that he needed to go to the ER.

After choking on his coffee, he agreed. We arrived at the Bay Pines VA ER with high expectations. Jim, who hates going to the doctors, was calm while we waited in the ER.

I and his daughters were more anxious.

We became inpatient and called his Neurologist while we were waiting in the ER. He explained the ER was full and there were no beds available. He did, however, get the staff to come out and administer an anti-seizure drug called Dilantin. After sitting in the ER for hours, I noticed Jim making unusual movements. His head went to the left and he seemed to be reaching for something. When I asked him what he was doing, he said, "I'm getting my medicine." He wasn't. I reported this to the nurse and told him that I thought he had another seizure. The nurse replied that would be good? Really, I was taken back by this statement. He replied "meaning I could move things along."

The picture is of Jim outside Bay Pines VA ER. He had been sitting in a wheelchair for hours. His legs were weak, as usual, but he wanted some fresh air and to stretch. You can see he was thin in this picture, at least to his family who knew him. Again, Jim's average weight was between 200 and 220 lbs.

They finally had a bed available in the ER. They gave Jim more medicine and he was finally able to sleep. They explained that they would be admitting him as soon as a bed came available in the hospital. At some point in the middle of the night, maybe 1 or 2 in the morning, we told the nurse we were going to lie down in the truck and to please call us when they got ready to move him to a room. They were kind and gave us a blanket since it was a cool October evening. We curled up in the truck trying to get our heads around what was happening, and to try and get a little sleep.

Approximately 5 or 5:30 in the morning, we got the call. Jim was being admitted and they had a room available. We stumbled into the ER to follow him up to his room. Jim was still calm and quiet. They got him situated in the room and brought in what only the military would have a "bed in a box." That's what they called it; they must have noticed how tired the girls and I looked. It was a small single mattress folded in a small box. We set it up and the girls laid down. The day was uneventful. The nurses did their assessment. Jim began to question why am I here?

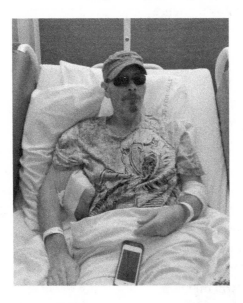

His eyes were bothering him and said the lights were bright, so he kept his sunglasses on. The the doctor on call made his round and we explained what was going on. The rest of the day was uneventful.

Somehow the girls and I all managed to sleep on the bed in a box. The next morning, I woke up to Jim rubbing the top of my head. As I looked up, I caught what could have only been a few moments. Jim's head was turned to the left and his hands began moving randomly across the hospital bed table they always give you. I asked, "What are you doing?" He tried to explain that he was reaching for something. There was nothing there for him to reach for. My gut told me that I had just witnessed another seizure, not like the grand mal seizure he had at home but a seizure I was sure. We reported it to the nurse.

A new Doctor came in to make rounds; again, we explained everything that had let up to Jim getting admitted, adding that we thought he had another seizure. She was curious and admitted to us that the nurse did not note the episode in his chart and that she wasn't sure what was going on. But, based on what we told her, she let Jim know he would not be going home. If my memory serves me right this would have been a Saturday. As the day progressed, we began to witness more episodes, seizures. They didn't last long but we witnessed the same symptoms; his head would turn to the left eyes too, and he couldn't recognize what happened.

The girls and I didn't leave his side. By Sunday, it finally got the nurses' attention. Jim had to use the restroom. I helped him as his legs, as usual, were not working well. As mentioned, earlier Jim had to sit down to urinate because of his bladder issues. He was standing next to the toilet and I was helping him lower his hospital pj's when to my surprise, he began to urinate. I looked at him but noticed the now familiar new symptoms. His head was turned, he was stiff and he was staring off into space. I pulled the emergency string you see in the hospital restrooms. A nurse came rushing in. About this time, Jim was coming back to us. I just reassured him and we helped get him changed. Now the nurses were coming in with bumper pads for his hospital bed and a urinal, along with an alarm on his bed. He was not to get up without assistance. They had started him on an anti-seizure med called Dilantin and now they were adding another called Keppra. I learned what he was having were tonic-clonic seizures.

Jim was getting restless and he couldn't recognize what was happening. We tried to explain and he would look at us like we were crazy. Luckily, the Doctor on call for the weekend was still serving in the military and Jim liked her and respected her. She didn't talk down to him and explained that they had to find out what was going on.

The picture is us getting Jim out of his room and cruising around the hallways.

He actually had another seizure while we were pushing him through the hallways. This time he became frustrated and asked what we were doing to him? What was going on? We didn't have the answers nor did we know this was in fact the calm before the storm.

Monday morning, the neurologist Jim had been seeing since moving to Florida was at the foot of the bed. I was happy to see him! He's a short, chubby older man with a New York accent. He was cheerful and asked what was going on. Again, we explained everything that had transpired in the last three days. As the Doctor was listening to us explain, Jim had another tonic-clonic seizure. He observed it and asked if that's what we had witnessed?

We said, "Yes, with the exception of the grand mal seizure he had at home."

He explained what anti-seizure meds he had given Jim and that they would be stopping the maintenance meds he had been on. Also, the neurologist ordered an MRI. Along with bloodwork, we waited patiently for test results hoping for answers.

The neurologist asked us to keep track of when and how long the seizures lasted. Also, he asked us to check and see if Jim remembers anything. He said, "As one is happening, tell him the name of a color." The Doctor left and we did as he asked. We started timing how long the seizures lasted and how far apart they were. We even tried the color test.

One happened. I yelled, "Red" After the seizure, I asked Jim if he knew what I said.

He said, "No"

I explained why I did that. The next seizure, I yelled, "Red." I asked Jim what color I said.

He replied, "Red!'

The next time the neurologist came in to check on Jim, we showed him our notes and how the seizures would last for seconds as they were coming closer together. I also told him of our color test. He laughed. He asked Jim if he knew what was happening or if he remembered the seizures?

Jim said, "No."

The Doctor said, "Try a different color next time. Jim was too smart for that." Over the next three days we documented over 450 tonic-clonic seizures. They were coming every few minutes lasting less than a minute in the beginning.

Not even realizing at the time, the girls and I hadn't had a shower. We were exhausted. It was all so surreal. When you're admitted to the hospital, most people get better. Jim was getting worse with each passing day.

Unbeknownst to us, the doctors were planning to move Jim to ICU. The seizures were lasting longer and coming closer together. As the nurse and staff came in to move Jim to ICU, they put him on a transport bed. I was following them when suddenly the wheel on the bed breaks! We are in the hallway and they are trying to radio for help. Jim besides having tonic-clonic seizures was still coherent in between the seizures. So, he begins to try and troubleshoot the wheel. He leans over the bed to check out the wheel. I thought the nurse was going to lose it. I laughed to myself. That's my guy, problem solver. Suddenly, there we were in a hallway between his old room and ICU, and he had another seizure!

They finally got him to ICU and got him settled into bed. Jim was not in pain, well except his usual back pain. He was actually calm. He didn't remember the seizures. He would come to with the three of us staring at him. He would reassure us, and say "don't freak-out."

His neurologist requested a family meeting. It was just the neurologist, me, his oldest daughter Jessica, and his youngest daughter Jennifer. Of course, it was a white sterile looking room with a large conference table. As we sat around the table, the doctor began to explain that they were giving Jim all the medicine they could and they did not know what was causing the seizures or why they would not stop! He went on to explain if the seizures continued or became worse, they would give him phenobarbital. But the amount they would have to give him to be effective could stop his breathing. If it came to this, they would have to intubate Jim. Again, it's not what you expect to hear. I didn't believe it would come to that. I expected Jim to get better. Why wouldn't he?

Our youngest had been researching CBD. She had read about the Realm of Caring. A company that had proven these oils were stopping seizures in children. It's known as charlotte's -web. She brought this up in the meeting with the doctor. I could see the terror on her face regarding her father's declining health. The feeling of helplessness, that there had to be more the doctors could do. The neurologist, while not disagreeing with her, said it wasn't something he could consider under the current laws. He went on to say the plan was to move Jim to Tampa VA hospital in the morning where they specialized in epilepsy.

We were exhausted. I think we were on day four and the three of us hadn't showered or slept but a few hours here and there. We were actually taking turns going out to our truck to lie down. I don't even remember eating. Looking back, I wish I could have been stronger for the girls. I should have made them leave and take care of themselves. But seeing how the nurse didn't document his seizure when he was first admitted and the negligence Jim had received in the past from the VA, we felt we had to be his advocate.

The nurses in the ICU were kind and took good care of Jim. They were even very concerned about us. I'm sure we were looking pretty rough by now, bloodshot eyes and all. The ICU Nurse brought us some juice and asked where we were staying? We explained we had been sleeping in the truck. The nurse explained that there was a place on the Hospital campus called the Fisher House we would have a room with a bathroom to stay in. It was a large home where patients' families could stay. There was a large kitchen, dining area and sitting area that guests would share. We were happy to hear this, but it was getting late and we couldn't speak with anyone until the next day. The nurses explained there was a shower and a kitchen on the hospice floor that we could use. We started to take turns taking a shower.

By now Jim's seizures were coming every few minutes. His left arm began to move uncontrollably. The nurse wrapped his arm because it was also where his IV was placed. I felt panic setting in. The nurse had our youngest daughter holding his arm down while he was seizing. Jessica the oldest walked in the room from getting a shower. She asked why Jennifer was holding Jim 's arm? Jim was getting worse and fast.

I didn't know it at the time but the nurse had already notified the neurologist. It was late in the evening. The next thing I knew Jim's neurologist along with another neurologist was in his room.

The doctor asked the nurse what meds Jim had been given and when. She hesitated; Jessica spoke up and rattled off every med, how much he was given and when he received the last dose. The room was quiet. The nurse spoke up and said, "She's a nurse."

Jessica added, "Do fucking something now! "Out of character for her but by then Jim was now having Grand mal seizures.

The doctor made the call! His neurologist told us, "You don't want to see this." They were about to intubate him. I had to force his youngest out of the room. We went to a small waiting area and collapsed. What was happening? We still had no answers as to why Jim started having seizures and why they wouldn't stop. Jim's brother showed up, about the time they were letting us back into the room. Jim was now intubated and in a medically induced coma. He was hooked up to an EEG too. His body was now still but they could see using the EEG that he was still seizing. His brother could see we needed to rest; he insisted we leave that he would stay with Jim. It had to be 1 or 2 in the morning by now. We found a way to a hotel for a quick shower and sleep in an actual bed. It felt good but I was anxious to get back to the hospital. We only slept a few hours and went back to the ICU to see if the seizures had stopped.

They hadn't. Jessica made arrangements for us to stay at the Fisher House. Jim's neurologist sat by his bed for hours. The nurses even commented they had never seen a Doctor do that. The girls also had to make some decisions. They both were employed. Not wanting to leave their dad's side, they filed for FMLA, the family medical leave act. Jessica also had a husband and three boys in Ohio to care for, but she couldn't leave until we had some answers.

Twenty-four hours after being intubated, on 3 antiseizure drugs and propofol, Jim's seizures finally stopped. They brought Jim up out of the coma, by stopping the propofol to do a neuro assessment. Jim was still intubated and couldn't open his eyes but was responding to the doctor's commands. He could move his legs and arms, a good sign the doctor told us. Jim was not breathing on his own; the machine was having to help. The doctor explained we want to get him breathing on his own as soon as possible because there is risk with being intubated. He was also too vulnerable to now be transported to Tampa VA Hospital.

Every morning a team of doctors would stand outside Jim's ICU room and receive a daily report from the nurse. I heard her begin to speak and she said, "He was vaccine injured from the Anthrax vaccine." I couldn't believe my ears. Finally, they heard Jim. I found out later Jim's neurologist had read the book *Vaccine-A* that Jim had given him. He was truly baffled by Jim's health problems and the course it had taken over the years leading up to the point where he became status epilepticus.

I went to Jim's bed side. I was so excited. I said, "Jim, they heard you. The doctor put in your file your vaccine injured!"

His neurologist would later and repeatedly put in Jim's records that he is vaccine injured from the Anthrax vaccine, and no longer list Multiple Sclerosis as his diagnosis.

The neurologist listed his disease of the brain as a demyelinating disease of the brain. While still in the hospital, Jim had an open claim for vaccine injury from the Anthrax vaccine. Because of his health, I submitted a claim to get a grant from the VA to make our home handicapped accessible. Guess what they told me. We cannot have two claims and the VA asked me to close his claim for Anthrax injury in order to pursue the rehab grant. We were later denied for this grant.

The next day Jim began to run a high fever. They were still trying to figure out what caused the seizures, now a high fever. They were running every test they could think of. Over the next few days, they fought to break the fever. It finally broke and they were able to also get him off the ventilator. They removed the vent and Jim's first word was "WOW!"

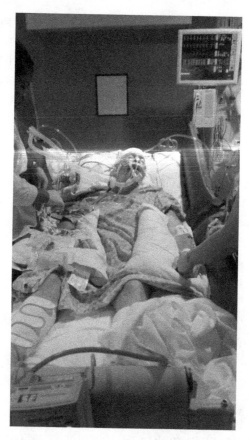

Pneumonia had set in, this was another hurdle. Jim could not walk nor swallow. He had a feeding tube through the nose, and he was catheterized. He was still losing weight. The neurologist came in to check on Jim every morning before he would start his day. The neurologist told us neuro assessments were good as far as following directions. He could see, and he could move his arms and legs. I was glad Jim's limbs were functioning and that he could see, but I knew he had a long road to recover. I was also noticing he was repeating himself, and would ask every few minutes, ``What time is it?" He is right-handed but was using his left hand. Prior to the seizures Jim watched a lot of news; he would ask repeatedly about ISIS.

Just a few things that I noticed in ICU, I mentioned to the doctor. He didn't seem too concerned. They told us the rehab unit there was full and that Jim would have to be transferred. They gave us a list of rehab centers. Our youngest Jennifer went the next day to look at the facilities. I imagined this great place with new technology that would get Jim back on his feet. We had doctors and nurses saying they had never seen a family like ours. I was taken back by the statement, not sure what they meant at first; they were referring to the fact we never left Jim alone. After they brought it to our attention, we began to notice how many Veterans were in ICU and the hospital that had no family or visitors. It was heart wrenching. Jim had always been a fighter and taught us well that the squeaky wheel gets the oil. He was still in bad shape and we were there to look after him and advocate for him, as he had always done for us.

Now that the seizures stopped and his pneumonia was getting better. We still had no answers as to why the seizures began. The MRI showed no new lesion; however, they stressed that Jim had innumerable lesions and brain atrophy. The neurologist even scheduled a time for our daughters to go to the radiologist office to view their dad's MRI's. I guess it was his way of trying to show how much brain damage was already there? They explained there could even be lesions that the MRI did not pick-up. The clonic-tonic seizures were affecting the right frontal lobe. Damage to this area affects executive functions. I will come back to this.

When Jennifer came back after visiting the different facilities, she was furious. She said "no way is dad going to any of those places; they are nursing homes with very little in the way of space or equipment for physical rehab." The doctor who saw Jim when he first came in heard that Jim had been moved to ICU. She came to see him. She couldn't believe he had declined so dramatically. She told us if he didn't have a strong heart he wouldn't have survived. She was a colonel in the Army, and Jim and she had made a connection when he was first admitted. We thanked her for believing us when we told her we witnessed the clonic-tonic seizure and because of that she didn't send him home. We told her about our concerns with getting Jim into a good rehab center. She said she would see what she could do.

They moved Jim to a private room. The neurologist explained they were buying some time until there was an opening in the rehab unit at their facility. We were very grateful. The girls and I were now rotating our time spent with Jim going to the Fisher house to shower, eat and sleep. It was walking distance from the hospital. A God sent to us, and many other family members; it was still a challenge.I would stay with Jim each night and we were now on two weeks in the hospital. Some things were beginning to improve for Jim; they were able to take the catheter out, and he could stand with help. They sent in a physical therapist to start working with Jim.

The rehab director came in and said they were working to get Jim moved to their floor. He couldn't walk without assistance and they had an alarm on his bed. They were still running tests trying to figure out why this happened.

Jim came back from having a scan and told me his kidneys were shutting down. I was perplexed at first. Most techs won't tell you anything. They wait for the doctor. Jim admitted this. When the doctor came, that was my first question. The doctor. said, "No, while his kidney function was affected from all the meds, they would be fine."

I reassured Jim that his kidneys were functioning and okay, but I was concerned. It wasn't like Jim. He started telling me we had to be quiet and that we were making the other patients mad because the tv was too loud. Jim was in the last room at the end of the hall. I reassured him we weren't bothering anyone. One of the times the physical therapist came in to walk Jim in the hallway, Jim started yelling out to another patient, "Hey, I'm sorry." He kept repeating this. The older gentlemen didn't notice. I asked Jim what was going on. He said he heard the other patients talking about him? The next odd thing was early in the morning. Jim was telling me he peed and it was running down the floor to the next level on other patients.

I again reassured him this didn't happen. He said he heard a man cussing and complaining about him. The next time his neurologist came in,

I expressed my concerns about Jim's mental health. He didn't seem to have any answers. I asked for a psychiatrist to come and see Jim. There were other things Jim was saying that were inappropriate and out of character for him. One of the nurses did tell me sometimes a person can get hospital psychosis, from being in the hospital long periods of time. I wasn't convinced; Jim was the most determined strong-willed man I've ever known. A psychiatrist finally came in and asked if he was hearing things.

Jim said, "Yes."

She asked, "Can you hear them now?"

"Yes."

She went with the usual psych. assessment, but left without answers.

The next hurdle was that Jim still had a NG tube (a tube that carries food through the nose). It was clogged. Jim was so skinny by now. The nurse came in and explained they were going to have to remove it and replace it. It was terrible they could not get it in place. Jim was still unable to swallow, so he could not help by swallowing. After what seemed like forever and him gaging. They stopped. I believe this was on a Friday. The speech therapist was coming in assessing him and giving him exercises to try to regain his ability to swallow. I was not happy. He was down to 145lbs. and was getting no nourishment. His labs reflected this as well.

By Sunday they were taking him in for surgery to put in a G-Tube, a tube inserted into the stomach to get nourishment. Jim was reluctant, to put it mildly, about having a G-tube put in. Looking back, we probably got lucky they listened to me and put one in. I did not have the medical power of attorney. He was pretty restless while waiting in the prep area and they asked me to come back. I stayed with him until they took him in for surgery.

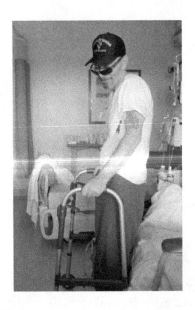 

The picture on the left is Jim in November 2014(he's only 50 in this pic), and the picture on the right was in 2006. Although he had health problems then, he maintained his weight and was a strong-looking man. I think that worked against him when he was trying to get answers. I know it did! The weight loss started slowly around late 2012 after an exacerbation. the doctors did not listen!

After the G-Tube was inserted, Jim was getting the nutrition he needed and I knew this would help with his recovery. I was still very concerned about his mental health.While Jim looks at me like I'm crazy, I again asked that he see a psychiatrist. Finally one comes in. It's a different doctor. That upset me. Now we have to explain what the family is seeing. Still no answers. They send another psychiatrist-- again a different one. She recommends we put him on Haldol!

I said "No,." I don't know if that was the right answer. I just couldn't imagine him having to be on drugs like this. I just wanted my husband back. I cried a lot that evening wondering if I made the right decision. I believed that his brain just like his body went through so much that he would come around, just like his body was starting to. They had restarted Jim's regular maintenance meds, minus the baclofen, tramadol, and Tecifidera used to treat MS. He was however on three anti-seizure meds: Phenobarbital (a really high dose), Dilantin and Keppra. Were these drugs causing his unusual behavior?

I was still asking the doctors, "Why?" "Why did this happen?"

One of the neurologists was a short, bearded, soft-spoken guy. He was the one in ICU who made the decision to intubate Jim. He said, "We don't know for sure, but it may have been a combination of things." He explained it to us this way. Think of your brain as having a brick wall that protects it. You take the brain damage, innumerable lesions that he already has, chronic pain, not sleeping, stress, and medications. All may have played a role in breaking down the brick wall allowing for the seizure activity. The only other answer was from the neurologist who had been following him and said he felt the Anthrax did something to him. He had never seen a case like Jim's.

We had to have faith and focus on getting Jim better. Jessica had to get back to Ohio to her family and work. Jennifer returned to work as well. My mom was still here, and thank goodness for her. She made sure we ate and kept up on our laundry, and of course offered moral support. One of the first times we left him alone for maybe 20 minutes, he fell while trying to get his phone. We were furious his bed alarm was not working. He was okay -- no broken bones.

Jennifer and I made the decision to make my first trip back to our home about 33 miles from the hospital. I had to get clothes and take care of a few household things. That was the day they decided to move Jim to the rehab floor. Jim wasn't having it. He didn't want to leave the room. He asked to speak to the Colonel. He made such a fuss they called the Colonel. She was actually headed out to the parking lot to go home for the day. She came back to the hospital to see what was going on? She was not even a part of Jim's care team at this point. But she went to his room, and later she told me how he was overwhelmed and just talked and talked to her about all sorts of things. She patiently listened while trying to coax him into moving rooms. Again, this was out of character for Jim. She finally convinced him to allow them to move him to another room.

Physical therapy began. Jim was receptive but I noticed right away he had trouble concentrating and following directions. I tried explaining to the therapist he was having trouble comprehending what they wanted him to do. He couldn't seem to count his reps. The loud noises and multiple patients in the therapy room seemed to be too much for him. I discussed this with the supervisor and things got a little better. They let me help count his reps and move him to the different stations.

Back in his room Jim was becoming paranoid; he had remembered that he had verbally fought with one of his siblings prior to being hospitalized. He didn't want to see him. I tried to reassure him he didn't have to see anyone. I came back to his room from a short break and saw a note on his door that said "No visitors allowed." I asked him what was going on and he said "I don't want my siblings or his family here." That was fine but again it was out of character for Jim to say he didn't want anyone coming in.

He was getting restless. With help he was able to get from the bed to a wheelchair, and his ability to swallow was coming back, he started using his right hand, but to this day he uses both his right and left hand. Every time the doctor came in, Jim asked to leave the hospital. They would remind him he had more work to do in physical therapy. He had now been in the hospital for four weeks. This did motivate him; he went every day and I could see him improving. He wanted to go home.

He was also becoming more paranoid that someone, even his family, would steal things from the house. We decided to have a security system with cameras installed at the house. I didn't think it was a terrible idea since at this point, I didn't know how much longer he would be in the hospital, and if it gave him reassurance and one less thing to worry about, I was getting it done.

After seven weeks in the hospital Jim was released to go home. He was able to eat, and he actually walked out of the hospital with the aid of a cane. I was so worried the seizures would start again, but he was home and we were all happy to be out of the hospital. The neurologist and his team were great, but they didn't have all the answers. They couldn't tell me if Jim would start to have seizures again. They only said that the longer he went without a seizure, the better odds he wouldn't have them again.

The next hurdle was Jim's mind. Physically he was improving but I was seeing all kinds of red flags. It was as if every bad thing that had ever happened to him, he was reliving. And he was imaging the worst of everyone. He even experienced confabulations; these are described as symptoms of brain damage or disease in which made-up stories fill in gaps of memory. A confabulation he had was; he began to tell me about a picture he drew while in the war. It was a picture of a fly, the size of an 8"1/2 by 12" paper. I had never seen this picture; he would get upset that I didn't remember and have me look for it. He was convinced a family member stole the picture. I don't doubt he drew this; it's just not one of things that made its way home, or was lost over the years. This became an ongoing battle; he wanted to file a police report. He even called the police once or twice to our home saying he was robbed. There was no convincing him this didn't happen. On another occasion we had a flat tire. He called the police and said a family member came to our home and put a nail in our tire. I explained the situation to the police and they were great about the call.

I went to each follow-up appointment with Jim. There were many. I expressed my concerns to his psychiatrist about his mental health, Jim was not in a good place and I was struggling to handle it. Of course, old marital issues came up too. Jim would even tell me often that I was fired (as his caregiver), especially when we would attend doctor appointments and I would try and discuss any new or worsening symptoms with his physical or mental health. His psychiatrist agreed to try Risperdal.

Jim's mood began to improve, but now he was having a huge decrease physically. He would wake up in the morning and say he couldn't move. We went to see his neurologist and he felt it was a side effect from the new drug. The psychiatrist agreed to change the medicine and put him on seroquel. His physical symptoms began to improve over time as we did a gradual change in the meds.

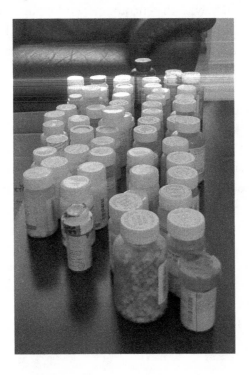

The picture depicts approximately sixty different prescriptions. This is what Jim had to endure after the seizures. This was not all at once: there were multiple changes in meds. I was begging the doctors for help because Jim was in a dark place. The new medication was not helping! The doctors seemed content that he came out of the seizures physically okay, but no one wanted to address the mental struggle he was enduring; a "mind storm". I will say the one exception was his neurologist; he heard me but insisted the mental health dept. should be handling this. But the psychiatrist just kept increasing the dose of the new drug. I struggled to figure out -- was it the drug causing Jim such mental anguish? Was there brain damage from the seizure? He did his best and after almost four years of hell, literally, Jim was weaned off two of the three anti-seizure meds and adjusted to new meds to help with anxiety.

Dealing with mental health issues is such a challenge for everyone involved-- mostly for the Veteran, but also for those of us who love and support them face many challenges and one of those is the red tape with the VA. I sought help with the encouragement of our daughters through the Veterans caregiver support line. One of the best lines from them was, "If he was having heart issues you wouldn't hesitate to force him to see a Dr." For those that are or who have dealt with mental illness it's very easy to get lost in their world. You must equip yourself with self -care and legal support.

Getting out and getting help is critical and a medical power-of-attorney can help, especially when the mental health doctor's advice was to seek out marriage counseling. I fired him! Jim's life will never be the same physically or mentally.What hasn't changed are the same reasons I fell in love with him, his determination and faith!

As we began to learn Jim's new normal, he was once again faced with a new challenge. He began to have trouble eating and even drinking. Choking on his food, I found myself having to perform the heimlich maneuver. The breaking point was on a typical day when he was eating dinner, chicken with a biscuit.

He began to choke. I jumped up and knew, unlike other times he could not clear it. I got him up and began to perform the heimlich maneuver. I managed to dial 911 on our cell phone, all while still performing the heimlich maneuver. 911 came on the line-- she could not hear me. I had to stop and get the phone closer. She got our address and said they were on their way. By now Jim could not stand any longer. He was close to passing out, and I could not hold him. He was still calm! I lost control of my bladder from the force I was using to try and clear his airway and realized Jim had too. I was sliding on the wet floor still trying to clear his airway. I laid him on the floor and put him on his side. In desperation with the phone in hand, 911 was still there. I ran to the neighbor's house and pounded on the door feeling panicked that I left him. I ran back home. Within minutes the neighbor was at the door. I yelle explained he was choking. He began to hit Jim on the back. His wife ran to another neighbor's house seeking help. I was assessing Jim and reached to his mouth and there was the piece of biscuit. I pulled it out. Jim came around; within minutes of this the ambulance arrived. Jim was starting to come around; they checked him out. Of course nothing obvious stood out and Jim refused to go to the hospital. I worked the phone and message system at the VA to explain to his doctors what happened. Once again his neurologist came through and Jim was scheduled quickly for surgery to exam his throat. The surgeon explained he has a presbyesophagus. What? The surgeon explained his esophagus was like a cork screw that also would spasm. There is no known cause or cure. Jim refuses to have the feeding tube put back in and lives on a soft food diet.

As we finish this book he asks me about every day, "Is it done yet?" He still faces many physical and cognitive challenges. The next month is full of scheduled tests that he swears are his last. He rarely complains and reminds me not to "freak out."

FAITH... I have struggled with this. There were many nights when I was on my knees asking God why? Why did Jim survive the seizures only to be tortured mentally? I begged him to give Jim peace. I swore I could handle anything physical, just help him find peace. Jim has never wavered-- not through our battle with his health, or our financial difficulties, or our battle with the Va and Va medical system. In June 2018, Jim was baptized. He was persistent about being baptized and thanks to our nephew Travis Anderss who is now no doubt an Angel in Heaven, Jim was baptized right here in our pool along with myself and our three grandsons!

Jim's MRI is back and the news is not good; the brain atrophy is now listed as severe. His brain is dying! It was like a kick to my stomach! Even though I had been witnessing the decline in Jim's health, I couldn't control my anger. The old memories and feelings came back. If only they had given Jim the MRI all those years ago! Could they have stopped or at least slowed the progression? I had to once again compartmentalize those feelings and be strong for him and me. The neurologist explained this is why we are seeing new and worsening symptoms. They have no cure and do not know what the future holds for Jim. I guess none of us do. Jim and I are left to face, accept, and adjust to this decline in his health.

As a type A personality Jim is very competitive, and I really struggle with finding a new challenge for his new sedate lifestyle, especially with the way this world is today, battling a pandemic! But I found a challenge: a 1,000 piece puzzle. It is an Army puzzle, no less, depicting a couple tanks, American flag, and soldiers. He lit up because he likes the challenge. Each day he says, "A 1,000 piece puzzle, really?" What was once easy is now complex in his world. I just encourage him and remind him he likes a challenge.

I've struggled with the ending to Jim's memoir, seeking some great accomplishment we could share. He completed a marathon or found hope in some wounded warriors program, or the stem cell therapy we went in debt for cured him. While the stem cell therapy helped his pain by 80%, it is not a cure. What we do hold onto is faith and family! And that "Time is the true currency". Jim has found some peace too. I thank God for every birthday, Thanksgiving, and Christmas that we celebrate. And of course I look forward to our next wedding anniversary. This year we will celebrate 37 years of marriage. We made it. All the silly things you argue about in a marriage seem so small now. One of our dreams as a young couple was to try and be good parents, offer them opportunities we didn't have, and grow old together. I think we have accomplished those goals.

In reflection I would say Jim and I are not naive to all the Veterans that have sacrificed so much! We know we are not alone in this battle and there are many that are still waiting for answers and compensation. Some may question his vaccine injury because not everyone who received the vaccine has suffered severe injury. Was it the perfect storm, mind storm for over 250,000 Gulf Veterans? I think so. We don't pretend to have the answers, but do believe the government has and still is experimenting with this vaccine. As far as guys in Jim's unit that took the vaccine that day, we have been unable to locate them. Jim does have a long-time Army buddy who did not go to war but suffers from Gulf War Illness. There are others that were in the theater and those that were not that have very similar symptoms. What is the common thread? We feel it's the vaccines.

Regardless of what you believe caused Jim's health problems, it does not excuse the treatment he received from the Veterans Administration. The health care system and compensation system to this day can be a nightmare for Veterans seeking help. There have been recent changes to the VA such as the VA Hotline, the Veterans Choice Program, and accountability of those working in the system who do not have the Veterans' best interest.

We know there are those in the system who care like his current neurologist, but sadly they are far and few between. We have found peace and realize what's important in life. It's the little things that matter and in the end your faith, family and friends are your true wealth! We can't thank our daughters enough for being there for us during these difficult times. They are too young to have to worry about caring for their parents. But, I truly believe because of their strength, Jim and I have once again been able to overcome the impossible!

Jim 2014 after eight weeks in hospital

2016 Jim, wife Melissa, daughter Jennifer, daughter Jessica, son–in–law Steve, grandsons Kaleb, Jacob, and Marcus.

"Ride to the Immortal"

The wings of eternity
Fly on the tip of time,
Like the
notes to a
song Of
unbalanced
rhyme...

Ready to be ridden,
Ready to be released
Ride through 10,000
Lifetimes...
Yet never cease

Spinning, whirling, descending,
Like a spiral
sea...
Unending

Sound & fury drown
All hearts,
Your every nerve is torn apart

Conquer your fears and
Whims so small...
Join the celestial souls
So great and tall...
Ride the wings of eternity.

A poem Jim wrote in high school, seems ironic now! As he tells me he
feels every nerve!

RESOURCES

We've listed some resources you or your loved ones may find helpful:

Gulf War Veteran Resource pages
https://gulfweb.org/

National Gulf War Resource Center http://www.ngwrc.org/

Provider Resources on
Gulf War Veterans Illnesses https://www.publichealth.va.gov/exposures/
gulfwar/pro viders/index.asp

We also recommend the book Vaccine A by Gary Matsumoto

https://images-na.ssl-imag es-amazon.com/images/I/4 1RXjQf3pHL.
SX326 BO1,204,203,200 .jpg

Whitehouse Hotline

https://www.va.gov/ve/whv   aHotline.asp#:~:text=White
%20House%20VA%20Hotl ine%3A%201-855-948-231 1.%20Calls%20
are%20ans wered,Veteran%2C%20mil itary%20family%20membe
r%2C%20caregiver%20or %20a%20survivor.

Below is a caregiver program for pre 911

Veterans Directed Care
Program (Formerly V-HCBS)

https://acl.gov/programs/ve teran-directed-home-and-c ommunity-based-services/ veteran-directed-home-co mmunity-based

Veterans Crisis line

https://www.veteranscrisisli ne.net/

Crisis hotline & blog for Caregivers

http://www.caregivingcafe. com/blog/2012/01/crisis-ho tlines-helplines/#:~:text=Fa mily%20Caregiver%20Allia nce%20%28FCA%29%201-800-445-8106%20Servic es%20for%20Family,Veter ans%20Affairs%20%28VA %29%20%E2%80%93%20National%20Caregiver%20Support%201-855-260-327

VA Caregiver Services

https://www.caregiver.va.g ov/support/support service s.asp

ABOUT THE AUTHOR

Staff Sergeant (SSG) James Sparks Jr., Honorable discharged from U.S. Army in June 1991, after eight and half years of service. Following the service to his Country he became a successful Tool Engineer. He currently reside with his wife in Holiday, Fl. Melissa Sparks, retired from the Social Services field after twenty plus years. And now devoted as his primary caregiver.